RELIGIOUS TOLERATION AND PERSECUTION IN ANCIENT ROME

RELIGIOUS TOLERATION AND PERSECUTION IN ANCIENT ROME

by
Simeon L. Guterman,
Ph.D.

GREENWOOD PRESS, PUBLISHERS
WESTPORT, CONNECTICUT

Originally published in 1951
by Aiglon Press Ltd., London

First Greenwood Reprinting 1971

Library of Congress Catalogue Card Number 70-104269

SBN 8371-3936-8

Printed in the United States of America

TO
MY FATHER
AND
MOTHER

TABLE OF CONTENTS

7

CHAPTER ONE

INTRODUCTION

THIS study is an attempt to find an answer to three distinct but closely related questions. Why were foreign, pagan cults under the Roman Republic sometimes tolerated, sometimes suppressed? Why was Christianity persecuted, at first sporadically, then systematically? Finally, why was Judaism generally tolerated?

The most comprehensive response to these queries has been given by Mommsen.[1] The pagan cults, otherwise unmolested, were occasionally repressed because they were disorderly or immoral, rather than because they were foreign. The Roman state took no notice of absence of faith on the part of the citizen; there was no *religionsfrevel* or religious crime under the late Republic. The votaries of foreign, pagan religions, by their acceptance of polytheism, did not incur the charge of atheism, the denial of the gods of the state.

Why were the Jews generally tolerated in the Empire?[2] And why the periodic persecutions? According to Mommsen, only the Jewish provincials were entitled to the privileges which formed the basis of the Jewish position in the Empire,[2a] because they formed a national group, or *natio*. Such persecution as occurred was directed against the Jews who were

Roman citizens. Not until the destruction of the Temple in A.D. 70, and after a temporary reduction to the status of *dediticii* brought about by their revolt, was Judaism opened to Roman citizens and then only to born Jews.[3] Judaism was thus a national cult attached to the Jewish *natio* before A.D. 70, and a religious confession, or *religio licita*, after that year.

Prior to the fateful year 70, therefore, the Roman citizens who practised Judaism were practising a foreign cult to which as citizens they had no right, a fact of which the Roman government occasionally took cognizance by expelling them from Rome.

Finally, why were the Christians, unlike the Jews, systematically persecuted ? Mommsen's solution of this problem forms the copestone of his ambitious thesis.

" The citizen of Rome," says Mommsen, " and even of any city of the Empire could not, at the same time, be a Jew and continue to belong to his city ; he could not recognize at the same time the gods of his country and the God of the Jews : apostasy from the national religion that polytheism did not imply, constituted, on the contrary, in regard to Jewish monotheism, the *crimen laesae religionis.*"[4]

And further on : " Even more categorically than the God of the Jews, the God of the Christians had no nation and did not suffer any other divinity at his side ; the community of the Christians has never been a political community and the Christian was necessarily an apostate from polytheism."[5]

It appears from these statements that Mommsen is advocating three propositions of varying merit. First, that the Roman state was essentially tolerant of foreign religions, provided that they were eclectic and were not practised by Roman citizens. Second, that Judaism

12

first presented the government with a problem of apostasy from the Roman national religion because of its severe exclusiveness, and that it was only saved from the fate reserved to Christianity by the fact that it had a *natio* (a political, ethnic, or geographic community) to legitimize its cult. Elsewhere Mommsen attempts to show that Roman suspicion of Judaism coincided with the growth within Judaism of a universal conception that was to blossom in Christianity.[6] Mommsen's third proposition is that Christianity was persecuted because it was both monotheistic and non-national.[6a]

Such is the theory of Mommsen, a theory based on a profound understanding of Roman statecraft, but one also revealing fundamental inconsistencies. If Roman policy, to select one instance, took no note of religious infidelity why should Jewish and Christian monotheism constitute a challenge to the gods of the state? But the most serious criticism of Mommsen's theory is that he fails to recognize the continuity in the government attitude toward foreign religions under the Republic and the Empire. For it is this author's contention that from the earliest incidents of so-called religious persecution recorded in Livy to the last great outbreak of persecution under Diocletian and his successors, an essentially uniform policy toward foreign cults was pursued by the government, a policy based on the requirements of the citizenship and the civic cult, and that the treatment of Jews, far from presenting an eccentric feature of this policy really formed an integral part of the government programme.[7]

The conclusions to which this study has led the author may therefore be briefly stated: (1) That the basis for the continuity in the Roman attitude toward foreign religions under the Republic and the Empire lay in the exigencies of the Roman citizenship and the civic religion. Roman citizenship was exclusive, that is, incompatible with the exercise of another citizenship.[8] The official Roman cult was exclusive ; membership in a foreign and unauthorized religion was barred to Roman citizens. " Every state has its own cult, *Laelius* ; we have ours," says Cicero.[9]

(2) That the religious crime, that is, the violation of the cult of the gods of Rome, still existed, albeit in a modified form, in the late Republic.

(3) That the foreign pagan cults were often repressed under the Republic because they were practised by Roman citizens and that it was precisely this practice which constituted the religious crime or *religionsfrevel*.

(4) That the Jews adapted themselves better to the classical conception of religion than the Christians because their religious organization was more national and less conspicuously given to proselytism and to doctrinal definition than the Christian.[9a]

(5) That Judaism was a *religio licita* before as well as after A.D. 70 in the western parts of the Empire where it was practised by Roman citizens.[9b]

(6) That Judaism was a national religion in the eastern parts of the Empire where it was practised by *peregrini*, or non-citizens.

(7) That the persecution of Christianity was a continuation on a greater scale, because it involved the infringement of the imperial as well as the civic cults, of the policy pursued under the Republic against foreign, pagan cults. Few students have remarked the coincidence between the policy announced by Septimius Severus in A.D. 202, of punishing Christian propaganda and the novel programme of political and religious integration enunciated in the Edict of Caracalla in A.D. 212.

By transforming the *peregrini* of the Roman Empire into citizens the emperor bestowed on his Christian subjects the dubious benefits of the Roman cult. The mutilated fragment of the papyrus which may contain the text of the ordinance seems to leave no doubt as to the emperor's preoccupation with the religious effects of the edict.[10] The inevitable accompaniment of this policy of political and religious assimilation in the Roman state was the outbreak of systematic persecution.

(8) That neither lack of nationality nor monotheism suffice by themselves to explain the Roman policy toward Christianity.

Couched in such terms this work may appear to be a study of Roman legalism were it not that the legal forms conceal a problem and a programme of vital importance to the modern as well as the ancient state. This problem revolves around the attitude toward religious dissent. The Roman policy toward foreign religions was one of religious toleration but of political intolerance stemming from the requirements of the civic and imperial cults. Whereas the intolerance of the Middle Ages was religious, that is, based directly on the pretensions of the Church or of the State to regulate the religious conscience of the individual, the intolerance of the Roman State was *political* and practical. It was based on the practice of foreign *sacra* by its citizens, or on the refusal by its provincial subjects to worship the image of the emperor. Minucius Felix expressed the difference between the ancient and the medieval view when he said to pagans : " You punish crimes actually committed ; among us even a thought may be a sin."[11] A modern writer's comment is, " The modern state reasons like the pagans, while the Church continues to reason like Minucius Felix."[12]

15

NOTES

(1) Th. Mommsen, " Der Religionsfrevel nach römischen Recht," in *Historische Zeitschrift*, 1890, LXIV, pp. 389 ff.; with greater precision and with several changes in detail the same view has been elaborated in Mommsen, *Römisches Strafrecht*, Leipzig, 1899, pp. 537–546, 567–580.

(2) Mommsen, T., *Historische Zeitschrift*, LXIV, 1890, pp. 421–426. Idem, *Rom. Straf.*, pp. 571–574. Juster, J., *Les Juifs dans l'empire romain. Leur condition, juridique, economique, et sociale* ; 2 vols., Paris, 1914.

(2a) Juster regards such toleration as a *privilegium* extended to Jewish Roman citizens. In one sense of the word a *privilegium* was an act of the legislative body directed at one person, or at one office, Maine, Henry, *Ancient Law* (Everyman's Library), London, 1931, p. 219. The Laws of the Twelve Tables forbade such *privilegia*, Strachan-Davidson, J., *Problems of the Roman Criminal Law*, 2 vols., Oxford, 1912, I, p. 26, N. 2, II, p. 41.—In private law a *privilegium* was a simple right of preference connected with a creditor, Beauchet, L., " Privilegium," *Dictionnaire des antiquités grecques et romaines*, Paris, 1877–1919, vol. IV, p. 657. There was also a *privilegium militum* which served to designate the special laws to which were subjected *milites* as opposed to *pagani*, who remained under the common law, Beauchet, *loc. cit.*, p. 658.—In all these instances the word *privilegium* assumes some form of legality.

(3) Mommsen, *Historische Zeitschrift*, LXIV, p. 425 ; Juster, *Les Juifs, II*, 15 ff. and E. Schurer, article, " Diaspora " in *Dictionary of the Bible*, ed. J. Hastings, New York, 1902, supplementary volume, p. 100 ff., both reject Mommsen's view. On *dediticii* in Egypt, see Van Groningen in *Aegyptus*, VII, 1926, pp. 189–202. For the basis of Mommsen's theory see *Digest*, 11, 7, 36 : " Cum loca capta sunt ab hostibus omnia desinunt religiosa vel sacra esse : sicut homines liberi in servitutem perveniunt." Mommsen, *loc. cit.*, in addition couples two facts with the Jewish status after 70 : the establishment of the *Fiscus Judaicus* and the disappear-

16

ance of a centralized Jewish community (thus giving rise to separate *collegia*); cf. Juster *op. cit.*, I, 419, who answers Mommsen on the latter point.

(4) Mommsen, *Strafrecht*, p. 573.

(5) Mommsen, *Op. Cit.*, p. 575. Cf. Paul Allard, " La Situation légale des Chrétiens pendant les deux premiers siècles," *Revue des questions historiques*, 1896, p. 8 : " Prier d'autres dieux etait permis, mais professer qu'eux seules avaient droit a l'adoration, qu'ils existaient seuls, etaient seuls vrais d'une vérité absolue parassait une attaque a la puissance romaine."

(6) Mommsen, *Strafrecht*, p. 573 : " . . . jüdischen Gemeinde aus einer nationalen in eine religiöse verwandelt . . ." For a different view see G. F. Moore, *Judaism in the First Centuries of the Christian Era*, Cambridge, 1930, vol. III, p. 17, who accepts the " continuity in the moral and religious teachings of normative Judaism."

(6a) For a criticism of several features of this view cf. C. Callewaert, " Les Premiers Chrétiens et l'accusation de lèse-majesté " in *Revue des questions historiques*, 1904, t. LXXVI, pp. 13 ff.

(7) Among the writers on this subject Le Blant, in his classic monograph, appears to accept such a continuity ; cf. " *Bases iuridiques des poursuites dirigées contre les martyrs,*" in *Les Persécuteurs et les martyrs aux premiers siècles de notre ère*, Paris, 1893, pp. 51 ff. : " Il ne parait pas que la legislation ait jamais varié sur ce point ; nous le voyons par le hideux episode des Bacchanales, dans les texte de Senèque . . . Ces deux crimes (la lèse-majesté, le sacrilège) etaient ceux des Chrétiens."

(8) See following chapter.

(9) *Pro Flacco*, XXVIII ; cf. also Symmachus, *Epistolae*, 10, 61 ; Macrobius, *Saturnalia*, 3, 9, 2 ; Tertullian, *Apologeticus*, ch. XXIV : " Unicuique etiam provinciae et civitati suus deus est . . ." See following chapter.

[9a] K. Lake, *Landmarks in the History of Early Christianity*, New York, 1922, p. 31.

[9b] The *religio licita* was probably recognised in Republican times, and was certainly confirmed and regulated by Caesar and Augustus, Josephus, *Ant. jud.* I, XVI, c. VI, 2 ; Philo, *Legatio ad caium*, 24. It is more difficult to set a *terminus ante quem*. The ill-fated Jewish risings of the period 120–135 may have affected the *religio licita*, but the author doubts it. Undoubtedly the Diaspora was more implicated in the revolt of 132–135 than in that of 66–70. The persecution of the Jews appears to have been temporary, though severe, according to Rabbinic writings. Dérembourg, *La Palestine au temps des Talmuds*, p. 430. The *privilegia odiosa* of the Christian Emperors seem to recognize Judaism as a cult rather than as a national system, Juster, *Les Juifs*, I, p. 253 : *Cod. Th.* XVI, IX, 4; XVI, VII, (" Nefanda superstitio," " Secta feralis "). The *religio licita* may, therefore, be said to have been sanctioned by the Roman authorities to almost the last days of the Empire.

[10] " Edit de Caracalla," *Dictionnaire d'archéologie chrétienne et de liturgie*, facicules XLI–XLII, cols. 2113 ff., gives the text of the Giessen Papyrus. For the religious significance of the edict see J. Stroux, *Philologus*, LXXXVIII, 1933, pp. 272 ff.

[11] Quoted by A. Bouché-Leclercq, *L'intolérance religieuse et la politique*, Paris, 1924, p. 348.

[12] *Ibid.*

CHAPTER TWO

ROMAN RELIGIOUS POLICY

Two problems present themselves for solution in connection with any study of the Jewish and Christian positions in Rome. The first is whether the citizenship of Rome was exclusive. The second is, Did Rome tolerate the practice of foreign *sacra* by members of its own citizen body? As has been suggested by both Mommsen and Juster, Rome, according to the strict letter of the law, would not have been able to tolerate the practice of Judaism by Roman citizens without some sort of *privilegium* if the former had been a national cult.

I. *Exclusive Character of Roman Citizenship.*

What was Rome's attitude towards double nationality? From earliest times to the latest, Roman law definitely forbade membership in foreign countries to any of its citizens.[1] The direct evidence for the rule comes from Cicero,[2] Nepos,[3] Gaius,[4] and it is implicit in the whole Roman law of exile; indeed, a goodly portion of public law is unintelligible without a clear comprehension of this principle. The following is from Cicero's oration for Balbus, "No citizen of ours may, according to the civil law, be a citizen of two states. . . . Oh Laws, prepared by our forebears, forbidding anyone to be a member of more than one state."[5] Cicero was evidently voicing the opinion prevalent among jurisconsults of his day, for Nepos recounts how Atticus refused the citizenship of Athens because many " jurisconsults regarded Roman citizenship as incompatible with any other."[6] The doubt expressed by Atticus, it appears to this author, was not on the score of the principle involved, but rather as to whether a city that was in subordinate relations with Rome was to be regarded as a free and equal state or not. For Rome, as the whole notion or *origo* attests, came to permit citizenship in two incommensurable political entities. Nepos was in the transition state when it was still impossible to say whether Roman citizenship would continue to remain merely the citizenship of the city of Rome or whether a larger citizenship of the Empire would supplant the older and more restricted civic concept.

A trace of the earliest obligations and liabilities of citizenship is retained in Gaius, " Formerly also, at the time when the Roman people used to send out colonies into the Latin districts, a man who by command of his ascendant set out for a Latin colony was regarded as exempt from *patria potestas*, since those who thus abandoned Roman citizenship were received as citizens of another state."[7] Here the older concept is stated, for even the subordinate relations in which a Latin colony necessarily stood to Rome did not enable a citizen of the latter to retain nationality in the mother city.

The doubt expressed by Atticus may have been echoed by the Greeks of Cyrene when they refused to incur the local *munera* in the belief that their Roman citizenship excused them from the duties of *peregrine* citizenship. Augustus, by refusing their petition, put the stamp of approval on the new imperialistic citizenship which was no longer incompatible with local, peregrine, citizenship, or *origo*.[8] When the latter contingency did materialize, the student finds himself in the presence of a slightly modified rule of citizenship, but one which in essential respects was similar to the older concept, for citizenship in an independent state other than Rome (Parthia, for example) was still regarded as incompatible with the exercise of Roman citizenship.[9]

Mommsen, the great oak upon which much of the science of Roman public law has been built, has put this fact very lucidly in the following words, "It is logically, and practically, as impossible to have at the same time several citizenships, or to belong at the same time to several cities, as to have simultaneously several fathers or several *gentes*, since the *gens* is as much the basis of the state as the home is the basis of the *gens* . . . the Romans in the Patrician as well as the Patricio-plebian constitution always remained, to the latest times, faithful to this principle which was founded on the very nature of things Roman, but which had been sometimes obscured by cases of honorary fictional citizenship. These have only mitigated in particular cases the rigorous consequences of the principle."[10]

Origo.

The Roman conception of citizenship is revealed in the notion of *origo*. Every Roman citizen, when the

Roman state had outgrown its earlier urban character, was presumed to have two allegiances, his Roman nationality and his municipal citizenship. The latter represented his *origo*.[11] The two, however, went hand in hand and one was often just as necessary as the other to filling out his legal personality.[12] *Origo* was concerned with the determination of such important matters as marriage, legal indebtedness, and city *munera*. When the individual became a citizen in a non-Roman state he lost his *origo* as well as his nationality.[13] *Origo*, in its origin, was undoubtedly exclusive in character, but it gradually outgrew this exclusiveness so that we find men with two *origines*.[14] Nevertheless, the fact that, in cases where a man possessed two *origines*, one was usually honorary, or fictional, would lead us to believe that the whole notion of *origo*, in common with that of *civitas* presupposed some form of incompatibility.[15]

For the imperial period, Mommsen predicates a relaxation of the principle of citizen–exclusiveness, which he identifies with the transformation of *civitas* into *municipium*.[16] In other words, when the foreign state, *civitas*, was no longer on a par with Rome, but was now only a part of the Roman *civitas* it was possible for a man to enjoy citizenship in these two otherwise incompatible political entities without injuring his status in one or the other. Mommsen's evidence for this view is in Augustus' military organization which made it possible for a soldier to partake of citizenship in two such cities as Capua and Ancyra. Mommsen admits, however, that Rome probably always regarded the exercise of its citizenship as incompatible with that of an independent state in treaty relations with it, such as Persia or Parthia.[17]

The Roman Law of Exile also Reveals Character of Citizenship.

There is good reason to believe that the principle of citizen-exclusiveness was not relaxed even under the Empire. Proof of this statement exists in the Roman law of exile.[18] The *ius exilii* was an institution to which the Roman citizen could appeal in order to escape or rather anticipate the consequences of a condemnation on a capital charge by a *quaestio perpetua*. According to Polybius, the accused was at liberty until the last vote had been cast in the Assembly to " depart openly, sentencing himself to voluntary exile ; and the banished man will be safe if he repairs to Tibur, Praeneste, or Neapolis, or any other state with which Rome has a sworn treaty."[19] The result of such a withdrawal is described by Mommsen, " Equally with the dead man there is excluded from Roman criminal procedure every man who is severed from the jurisdiction of Rome. Now since every Roman citizen is subject to that jurisdiction even when he happens to be abroad and every foreigner is so subject when he happens to be on Roman territory, it follows that the only persons excluded are foreigners who live abroad, and the Roman citizen can withdraw himself from it only if on the one hand he quits Roman soil (*solum vertere*) and on the other hand attaches himself to some state whose independence is formally recognized by Rome, as a citizen or in such a way that his reception into it annihilates his Roman Citizenship."[20]

It is furthermore clear from Polybius, Cicero, and Sallust that the loss of citizenship was not the punishment but the consequence of admission to the citizenship of another state. Roman citizenship could be surrendered voluntarily by assuming a foreign nationality ; it could not be taken away by force.[21] There is little doubt, also, from the words of Cicero, that the *interdictio aquae et ignis*, the new form which the death penalty assumed under Sulla, did not abolish the *exilium* mentioned by Polybius in favour of *relegatio*, or the forced banishment of a Roman citizen from Italy, a penalty which was not supposed to entail the loss of citizenship.[22] Clodius asked Cicero on his return, " Cuius civitatis es ? " because it was well known that the consequence of exile was usually that the accused, in order to save himself, assumed the citizenship of another state and thus cancelled his Roman nationality.[23]

The principle of citizen-exclusiveness was so firmly intrenched in Roman law that the return of exiles was regarded as one of the horrors of revolution.[24]

Cicero's friend, the jurist Servius Sulpicius, as a member of Caesar's Senate in 49 B.C., threatened to leave Rome if a wholesale *exulum reditus* were decreed by the Senate.[25] Tiberius was the first in A.D. 23 to abolish the old *exilium* and, in defiance of the rule of Cicero, to take away the Roman citizenship of the accused without demanding some act on the part of the latter to cancel it.[26] We know that during the reign of Augustus the old *ius exilii* was still in existence, for Ovid, in a few pithy lines, contrasts the position of the *exul* who lost his citizenship with that of the *relegatus* who was spared this fate.[27] When with Tiberius, therefore, *deportatio* supplanted the Sullan *aquae et ignis interdictio*, " the opposition between *exul* and *relegatus* was continued in the opposition between the *deportatus* and the *relegatus*."[28] Whereas deportation, connected with the old notion of *exilium*, involved the loss of citizenship, *relegatio* did not. Here we have good proof

24

that after, as well as before the time of Tiberius, the whole institution of what was roughly called exile still bore the imprint of the principle of citizen-exclusiveness. It was no longer possible " to shake the soil for exile," (solum vertere exilii causa), for no city could be found at that time in treaty relations with Rome, and yet independent, so that reception by it could cancel the Roman citizenship of the accused, but within a sphere thus circumscribed the old concept of citizenship continued to apply.[29]

II. Roman Religion in Relation to Citizenship.

The transition from the general conception of *civitas* to that of the *sacra*, or religion, is not difficult to make on *a priori* grounds, for the two were very closely linked. To speak of the gods was to speak of " the gods of Rome, a sort of highest class of Roman citizens. As such they had, one might almost say, their duties toward the state while the state, for its part, was obliged to provide them with their proper offerings and honours. There is a total lack in the early Roman cult of that often unmanly humility in the presence of objects of adoration which meets us in Semitic worship ; the Romans and their gods are rather in the position of free contracting parties."[30] It is little wonder that the Romans up to the latest times ascribed their success as a people to the fidelity with which they observed the conditions of this contract with the gods.[31] Augustus was actuated by civic as well as religious motives when he restored worship in Italy after it had fallen into desuetude.[32]

Roman religion, therefore, true to its political character, early found itself mingled with two developments in Roman history, imperialism outside the city and the struggle of the orders within the state. It was probably under Etruscan auspices that a religion of patriotism supplanted the religion of physical increase which had formerly existed in Latium.[33] The cult of Jupiter Optimus Maximus on the Capitoline, the temple on the Alban mount that later became the centre of the Latin league, and the *pomoerium*, the sacred boundary of the City of Rome, all attest the religio-civic basis of the movement that was to lead to the conquest of Italy.[34] Within the state religion early became a millstone in the struggle of the plebeians for admission to public office.[35] The argument of the patricians, " auspicia non habetis," agreed, in the emphasis which is put on religion with the terms Caracalla employed in his grant of *Citizenship to Peregrini*.[36] Not only was religion closely linked to politics but it influenced the life of the state in other ways. In the realm of law it early seized on certain offences and made " sins " of them.[37] The *homo sacer* survived in the *interdictus aquae et ignis*.[38] Religion brought international relations within the field of the *ius fetiale*.[39] In fact, subject to certain limits, much of the later secular law or *ius* may be said to be descended from *fas*, or religious law.[40]

The fact that Roman religion was political did not mean that it was only public ; it had its private side also. The pontiffs saw to it that no ancestral rite was ever neglected.[41] As such they had to regulate *sacra privata* as well as *sacra publica*.[42] Unlike other religious states the Roman made little distinction between public and private worship; the same rules apparently applied to both.[43] From these facts it becomes clear that religion and citizenship had similar bases and that one may be justified in applying the rules learned in one to the other.[44]

26

III. The Problem of New Divinities.

Roman religion and the Roman pantheon were not static. They underwent development and enlargement in accordance with the needs of each age. Neglecting other phases of this evolution we may well ask what principle governed the admission of new deities to the state. Let us beware at the outset of that hypothesis that makes Roman policy a result of a toleration supposed to be implicit in the polytheistic fabric of ancient religion. If we understand by toleration a " laissez faire " attitude toward the religious cults of foreigners, the word may well convey an accurate picture of Roman policy. If, however, by toleration, we understand assimilativeness we shall be deceived, for the Roman government's position on foreign cults was selective rather than assimilative.

Various causes impelled the Roman state to admit new gods. Sometimes conquest resulted in the transfer of the deity of a conquered city to the Pantheon. Such were the antecedents of Juno of Veii, and of Juturna of Lavinium.[45] At other times new deities were adopted to keep pace with the increasing concerns of a developing culture, as when Neptune was identified with Poseidon as a form of " marine insurance," or as when the first use of silver money led to the adoption of its patron god, Argentinus.[46] But more often it was public disaster that brought about the incorporation, as was true of Cybele during the second Punic War.[47]

On another occasion, as a result of a plague, the Sibylline Books were consulted and the worship of Aesculapius introduced from Epidaurus.[48] It would be futile to attempt to find a guiding principle in this

27

development; it was fortuitous and accidental. Tertullian and Arnobius have some such thing in mind when they write respectively, "With you it is the whim of man which determines divinity. If a god hasn't pleased some man, he will not be a god "; or Arnobius, "If anyone therefore asked you why you have so lately undertaken the worship of these divinities, it is certain that you would answer, either because we did not know that they were among the gods or because we were warned by our prophets or because we were saved by their help from misfortune."(49)

If the causes that led to the adoption of new deities were accidental, the same cannot be said of the process and result.

Process Typically Roman.

As regards the process, it should be clear that there existed a body within the state which dealt with the claims of divinities for recognition. This organ was the senate. The senate's policy in regard to religion was conservative.(50) We shall attempt presently to show that the result of this policy was to compel a Roman citizen to confine himself to the worship of the gods of the state. In a state in which religion and citizenship were so closely linked, it was not strange that a citizen's religion as well as his civic life, should be so controlled.

As regards the result, the whole picture is also typically Roman. A distinction was made between the *Di novensiles*, the newly admitted divinities, and the *Di indigetes*, the old gods.(51) Only the latter were to be admitted within the *pomoerium*, or sacred boundary, but the worship of both was permitted.[52] The Roman passion for classification is also revealed in Varro's distinction between the *Di certi* and *Di incerti*.[53] Festus' distinction between the gods admitted during war by *evocatio* and those admitted in peace *ob quasdam religiones* is probably based on the differing origin of each group of gods.[54] It was assumed in all cases that the god, by being admitted to Rome, lost his former nationality and became strictly Roman.

An interesting pendant to this fact was the Roman law in reference to *locus religiosus*. If the tomb of a Roman fell into the hands of the enemy, all *religio*, or religious sanctity vanished from it.[55] This attitude has been contrasted with the respect shown by the Greeks to foreign heroes, " together with their anxiety to get the bones of their own if they lay in foreign soil."[56]

IV. The Private Citizen and the Worship of Unauthorized Divinities.

Was the Roman citizen permitted to worship gods other than those approved by the state, provided that this worship was carried on in private ? There is little doubt that a magistrate was not allowed this liberty, but that this interdict applied also to private worship by citizens has been a bone of contention among students. Boissier has thus put the question, " But these gods that were not consecrated, that is, that the state had not officially recognised, might they be worshipped by private citizens at home ? A passage of Cicero seems to establish that it was no more permitted to raise an altar to them in one's own home than to dedicate to them a temple on a street or a public place. Livy, on the other hand, confines the interdict to sacred or public lands ; it was there only, according to him, that the citizen was forbidden to sacrifice according to foreign rites. One cannot explain this difference between two writers ordinarily well informed except to suppose that the law was not often enforced in its rigour."[57] While the problem that Boissier poses here is legitimate, it is doubtful whether one may found it on the two passages cited.

The statement of Cicero is as follows, " Let no one have gods separately ; nor let them cultivate in private new and strange gods unless publicly summoned."[58] Later on in the same tract, Cicero remarks, " What follows concerns not only religion, but the general order of the state ; namely, the prohibition which restrains private individuals from offering sacrifices without the superintendence of the public ministers of religion."[59] The words of Livy which Boissier has opposed to the preceding are, " A task was given by the senate to the urban praetor, Marcus Aemilius, namely, that he free the people of religious rites (*eis religionibus*) and he ordered (*edixit*) that no one should sacrifice by a new or foreign rite in a public or sacred place."[60] To take this ruling as an interdict directed only against public worship in general is to exaggerate its import which was definite and aimed at certain acts that had given the government concern. Furthermore, a sacred place could be private as well as public. The edict must therefore be understood to have forbidden private as well as public worship of strange gods. Indeed, the statement Livy has made elsewhere is sufficient warrant of the accuracy of such a version of the praetor's ruling.[61]

Evidence Showing that Such Worship was Forbidden.

Quite definite on this question are the words Dio puts into the mouth of Maecenas. The latter was haranguing Augustus on his duties, in the year 29 B.C. " Therefore, if you desire to become in very truth immortal, act in this way, following our fathers' belief and compel others to honour it. Those who introduce strange ideas about it you should both hate and punish not only for the sake of the gods, but because such persons, by bringing in new divinities persuade many to adopt foreign principles of law from which spring up conspiracies . . ."[62] Here Maecenas not only had in mind the duty of a magistrate to see that public worship was maintained pure but the further duty of keeping citizens from foreign deities. Otherwise, why the objection to having many " follow foreign principles of law?" Hence the liability of those who brought in foreign cults extended not only to adulterating the purity of the public cult but to weaning private citizens away from it. Maecenas's words refer not only to practice in public but also to practice in private, for it was from private practice particularly that " conspiracies " arose. Moreover, the introduction by a magistrate of novelties in the religion of the state or vice versa, his neglect of the state cult, were from early times crimes punishable *per se*.[63] The well-known instance of Marcus Scaurus provides an example of a charge against a magistrate based on his neglect of the cult of the Penates.[64] So that Dio cannot be referring only to the responsibility of magistrates, a responsibility that was fixed in law, but must have also included the responsibility of private individuals who spread unlicensed religion among the people.

The rule is further illustrated by two statements from the jurisconsults that look as if they supplemented the words of Maecenas. One is that of Paul, " Those who introduce new kinds of worship, unknown to custom or reason, and thus disturbing weaker minds, are to be punished, if persons of rank, with deportation ; if not of rank, with death."[65]

The other jurisconsult is Modestinus : " If a person has caused the minds of men to be in superstitious fear of a deity the divine Marcus has decreed that such a person be deported to an island."[66] It is difficult to say whether Modestinus employs the word " superstitio " in its proper legal sense of something superfluous, exaggerated, or in its religious sense of credulity, magic.[67] The gap, however, between these senses of the word was never great and the term was often used indiscriminately to refer to foreign, unauthorized religion.[68] That there may have been an old law which struck equally at sorcery and at foreign rites is not improbable ; if such is the case, we have in the rule of Modestinus the imperial counterpart of the old *incantatio mali carminis* of the Twelve Tables.[69]

Cicero echoes the sentiment of Dio when he says, " And for individuals to worship private gods or new gods or strange gods, would introduce a confusion of religions and all kinds of unknown ceremonies."[70] It appears as if Cicero and Dio were reciting from the same manual.

At any rate, here in a passage from a work that was undoubtedly inspired if not based on Roman law, we find the statement that no " individuals may worship private gods."[71]

Dionysius has given us what may well be regarded as the practical commentary on these texts from Livy,

Cicero, Dio, Tertullian. He states, "And what I admire above all things, notwithstanding the resort of innumerable nations to Rome who are under a necessity of worshipping their own gods according to the custom of their respective countries; the commonwealth has never, by public authority, adopted any of these foreign institutions; a misfortune many other cities have fallen into: but if, pursuant to some oracle any images of the gods have been brought thither from foreign nations, they honour them according to their rites, banishing all fabulous impostures, and, in this manner, they worship the image of the Idaean goddess. For the praetors performed annual sacrifices and celebrate annual games in honour of her, according to the Roman customs; but the priest and priestess of their goddess are Phrygians. These carry her image in procession about the city . . . but no Roman born is, by any law or ordinance of the Senate, obliged to walk in procession . . . so fearful are they of admitting any foreign customs in religion."[72]

This passage is of interest from several points of view. In the first place it indicates how a cult which had been officially admitted by the government was nevertheless subjected to various restrictions that (and this is its second interest) prevented a citizen from participating in its ceremonies. The explanation of this fact seems to be that government policy in regard to foreign religions suffered occasional change.

We shall see later that Judaism, though a licensed religion, also underwent vicissitudes in its relations with the government. It is only on this assumption that we may explain the existence among numerous other cases of an Archigallus of Cybele who was a Roman citizen.[73] There is no need to suppose that

33

Dionysius was indulging a passion for antiquarian lore when he states that a Roman citizen could not participate in the processions of Cybele, though there is more truth in the view that his words echo a plank of the Augustan Restoration that was itself the product of tradition.[74]

V. Existence of a Law Punishing such Worship is Disputed.

There is little doubt that the evidence thus far cited can lead to only one conclusion : that the practise of unauthorized rites was forbidden to Roman citizens. But though this first proposition may be stated with confidence, it is not with the same confidence that one may state its corollary, namely, that the government in historic times applied a sanction for violation of the rule.[75] Yet without such a sanction it is doubtful whether we can predicate the existence of a *law*.[76] Scholars with few exceptions deny the existence of a religious crime, or *religionsfrevel*, at least during the mature Republic and early Empire.[77] It is contended that if there ever was such a crime, it suffered the same fate as the religious tribunal which was first invested with its enforcement, namely obsolescence.[78] Some colour is supposed to be lent to this view by the absence of any tests, such as sacrifice or the recitation of a catechism in the Republic, by means of which a Roman citizen might be checked on his conformance to the cult.[79]

The supposed absence of a *crimen laesae religionis* is the more remarkable by comparison with the system in Athens where religion and politics were not otherwise so closely linked.[80] Yet in Athens *Asebeia* had an established formula of accusation which, though it was at first based on the actions of a citizen, was extended to cope with expressions of unorthodox thought.[81] It was in accordance with this rule that Anaxagoras and Socrates were convicted and sentenced.[82]

If we look further afield for some explanation of this anomaly and ask whether the civil jurisdiction might not have taken over the religious crime to its own cognizance we are usually met, in answer, with the words of Tiberius, " *Deorum injurias, diis curae.*"[83]

Explanation Given by Mommsen of Suppression or Foreign Religions.

How are we to explain the numerous suppressions of foreign religions in the Republic and early Empire? Mommsen has given what is the generally accepted answer by making these prosecutions consist of nothing more than magisterial interventions in behalf of public order, thus denying that in any or all cases of such conflict was there any criminal trial.[84] It was not until the growth of Christianity that the government had to establish a religious crime.[85] It is worth noting that the crime that was thus defined was not based on a violation of the old religion of the state, but on that of the new religion of the Empire which consisted essentially in the worship of the Emperor, living or dead.[86] The *religionsfrevel* which Mommsen predicates for the later period was not strictly speaking a crime against the civic order, for it was based on the universality rather than the nationality of the offending cult.

This, in outline, is the picture which is drawn for us by contemporary students. Before we discuss its other features it will be necessary to examine the historical evidence on which it rests with a view to ascertaining how far motives of public order or morality actuated the government in its repressions of foreign cults, and whether any trial procedure was employed in these prosecutions.

The Historical Facts.

Our first instances are recorded by Livy. In 425 B.C., owing to a contagion, superstitions spread through the city with the result that "foreign and unwonted expiatory offerings" (*peregrina atque insolita piacula*) were made to the gods.[87] The complaint here is the practice of unwonted *sacra*. There is no mention of immoral practices. The order given to the aediles on this occasion does this point justice. They are told to see that "no god except Roman be worshipped in no manner other than the Roman." These instructions obviously applied to private citizens as well as to magistrates, and we may thus again ignore any possible distinction between the practice of public and private religion. Another incident mentioned by Livy also resulted in the praetors being requested to see to it that "no one should sacrifice in a public or sacred place by means of a new or foreign rite."[88] Here also the objection to the strange worship was that it was " externa." No reference is made to immoral practices, and if Livy with the tendency common to most writers of his age of painting his pictures sensationally does not mention it we may again ignore such

36

a possibility. Finally, from Livy we glean a remarkable speech by the consul Decius that sums up the whole Roman theory on the matter. When people were alarmed lest they violate " any divine law by punishing human fraud in religion " the consul reassured them in the following words, " Innumerable decrees of the pontiffs, of the Senate and the responses of the *haruspices* release you from such scruples. How often in the age of our fathers and our grandfathers was the task given the magistrates to forbid the practice of foreign rites (*ut sacra externa fieri vetarent*), to prohibit sacrificers and diviners from the forum, from the circus, from the city, to seek out and burn all prophetic books, to abolish every type of sacrifice except that approved by Roman custom (*præterquam more romano*)."[89] It is worth noting that magic is put in the same class of crime here with the practice of foreign rites. This fact is of especial interest in the Bacchanalian Affair, in connection with which this speech was given, and which seems to reveal, as none of the other incidents mentioned by Livy do, a motive of public order or morality. Either Decius' remarks on this occasion were irrelevant or the same rubric included crimes against public morals and public religion.

Whatever the legal basis of the Bacchanalian prosecution, whether the votaries of this sect were suppressed on the basis of a law against nocturnal associations[90] or secret reunions[91] or of *incantatio mali carminis*[92] there is no doubt that the main motive was public order and concern about political conspiracy.[93] In its original form, as practised in Magna Græcia, the cult was free of those orgiastic elements that were engrafted on it by Etruscan influences in Rome.[94] The cult of Bacchus itself was licensed from the first, and, as inscriptions attest, continued to exist after the prosecution; it was obviously only in its public or orgiastic form that it was suppressed.[95]

The distinction which is sometimes made between religious practice in public and practice in private oversteps the bounds when it appeals for evidence of such a distinction to that provision of the Senate's decree permitting small groups with the permission of the prætor to discharge the rites of the cult, for another provision expressly forbids private as well as public celebration without the necessary permission.[96] There is also little doubt that the sect must have been regarded as a source of conspiracy from the way in which the Senate and magistrates proceeded to override all ordinary constitutional safeguards such as *provocatio*, and the distinction between citizen and non-citizen.[97] The political nature of the whole affair is indicated by the rising that followed in the wake of the Senate's decree: in 184 B.C. the prætor, Lucius Postumius, broke up an army of shepherds near Tarentum; in 181 B.C. Duranius continued the inquests in Apulia.[98] " Le Sénat devait craindre une coalition du monde héllenique et l'Italie méridionale, en Campanie et à Rome."[99]

It is difficult to find religious motives in any part of the affair unless, as we have suggested, one crime included offences against public order and against religion. In view of such a possibility it may be well to note several points about the affair that would otherwise call for no mention. First are the trials which were apparently conducted without recourse or appeal to the people and thus appear to violate a fundamental principle of the criminal law.[100] They thus resemble prosecutions for the later crime of *Maiestas*, which also deprived a Roman citizen of all privileges.[101]   It does not appear likely, however, that the Senate and the magistrates exceeded their powers when they conducted such trials.   It is more likely that here we have an instance of the *ius coercitionis* of the magistrates functioning in all its plenitude.   Equally worthy of note is the penalty inflicted, which was death.[102]   The peculiar manner in which women implicated were tried, namely, by a household trial, may be compared with the later trial of Pomponia Græcina.[103]   This is no more strange than the irregularity with which the whole affair was conducted from the point of view of the regular criminal law.

In 139 B.C. according to Valerius Maximus, the Jews were expelled from Rome because they " were trying to infect customs (*inficere mores*)."[103a]   The same fragment suggests a confusion between the Jewish God and the Phrygian Jupiter Sabazius.[104]   It is not impossible that such a confusion actually took place as a result of the activity of Hellenizing Jewish sects.[105]   The objection to these Jews was probably not the practice of immoral or disorderly rites as was the case with the Bacchanalians, but simply their proselytizing activities.[106]   Judaism was at that time a foreign, unlicensed cult, and therefore forbidden to Roman citizens.

Pomponia Græcina.

When we turn to the case of Pomponia Græcina, we find that the charge on which she was turned over to her husband for trial and found innocent was *superstitio externa*.[107]   It has been suggested that the charge was one of adultery, but the words of Tacitus themselves only affirm that Pomponia was practising foreign religious rites.[108] That Pomponia was a Christian has also been urged on the basis of inscriptions of a century and a half later that refer to Pomponius Græcinus and Pomponius Bassus.[109] Whatever the case about Pomponia's Christianity, two things appear to be well founded; that she was tried on a charge of practising foreign rites and that this was a capital charge. Strictly speaking, only a woman in the *potestas* or *manus* of a husband or father might be thus tried, but the undeveloped character of the Roman criminal law is shown by the fact that women *sui juris*, that is, women independent of such control, were similarly tried and even executed.[110] This is presumed to be a survival from " original order of things according to which a woman always and necessarily remained under *patria potestas*."[111]

A number of cases under the Empire not concerned with Christianity reveal a religious basis. We are neglecting for the while such incidents as the conscription of the Jews under Tiberius and their " expulsion " under Claudius as well as the measures against cults like Isis, which are to be interpreted as mere actions of the government against public disorder.[112] The incident of the accusation of Flavius Clemens on a charge of atheism (αθεοτηζ) raises the question whether Dio speaks here as a jurist or not.[113] Mommsen believes that *atheotes* was the literal Greek rendering of the Latin *sacrilegium* and that the word was therefore devoid of a juristic sense.[114] It is likely, as we shall point out below, that *sacrilegium* had a much wider connotation in law than has been commonly ascribed to it.[115] Flavius Clemens was therefore practising a religion not approved by the state and his crime was aggravated by the fact that he was consul.

Conclusions.

Let us attempt a few conclusions to this account. In nearly all cases cited, with the exception of the one involving the Bacchanalians, the charge pressed was the practice of *sacra externa*, or some variant. The procedure differed. It might take the form of a household trial as in the case of the Bacchanalian women and of Pomponia Græcina. It might take the form of an inquest by senatorial commissions and magistrates, as in the affair of 180 B.C. Or again there might not be a criminal trial at all ; there might be simple expulsion of the offenders, if they were foreigners. We know from the treatment of Christianity that the government was always lenient in the event of recantation on the part of the accused, though political exigencies might aggravate the state's conduct.[116] The absence of public trials or the irregularity of procedure does not preclude the existence of a religious crime that might have served as a precedent for the persecution of Christianity.

VI. The Persecution of Christianity in Relation to Previous Persecutions.

When we investigate the situation of Christianity, we are struck by the resemblance it offers to that of some of the cults which were suppressed in the Republic. It is not our purpose to venture another solution to the much mooted question of how the Roman government legally persecuted Christianity, *in the first two centuries of our era*, whether by means of the *jus coercitionis* of the magistrates, or on the basis of the ordinary criminal laws in existence, or on the foundation of a special law forbidding the practise of Christianity. We shall merely point out in what way the government policy when completed followed the general lines laid down during the government's struggle with religious offences in an earlier period.[117]

Mommsen's hypothesis that an excess of monotheism and a deficiency of nationalism provoked the policy of persecution against Christianity is not based on an old principle of Roman law but on a new idea non-existent before the advent of Christianity. Roman policy was practical, not philosophical; only a philosophical or theological system could have bridged the gap in thought involved in saying that the acceptance of a single god entailed the denial of the existence of other gods. The experience of the apostle Paul, as recounted in Acts, shows that the Roman governors were ignorant of the implications of monotheism (as understood by Mommsen) at least during the earlier period.[118] If we examine the obverse side of the monotheistic hypothesis and ask whether the lack of nationality might have provoked government interference, we may well answer by asking in turn why the government should have taken notice of one schismatic sect in Judaism and have ignored others. Why was Christianity any worse off in this regard than Zealotry and its religious expression, Pharisaism, which, so far as the government was concerned, constituted a greater political danger? If we attempt to draw a line of demarcation between Judaism and Christianity for juristic purposes on the basis of the latter's proselytizing policy, we are in danger of forgetting that Judaism was in this period also guilty of much proselytism.[119] If we judge from certain obvious facts, such as the dispersion of population, Judaism was anything but a regional or national system in this period.[120] The view that makes Christianity represent the efflorescence of the universalistic tendencies in Judaism, and Pharisaism the repository of all the older nationalistic ideas, a view which appears to be at the basis of Mommsen's theory, may to a great extent be discounted.[121] The more we learn about Pharisaism, the smaller the gulf appears between its tenets and those of nascent Christianity, which at the outset certainly shared with Judaism some nationalistic bias.[122] The words of the governor, Gallio, at one of Paul's hearings probably reflect the Roman government's attitude, " I am here to execute Roman law, settle for yourselves points of doctrine."[123]

The Theory Does Not Make Sufficient Provision for Cives Romani.

The nationalistic hypothesis also makes insufficient provision for the two great categories of Roman subjects, *cives* and *peregrini*, and the distinction between them. If the new crime of *religionsfrevel* arose out of the violation of the cult of the Emperor, then it could not have affected Roman citizens who were but imperfectly implicated in Cæsar-worship on the Italian peninsula. This new crime would have affected *peregrini* who alone were subject to the cult of the Emperor.[124] But there had been, for centuries before this time, a civic religion involving Roman citizens which continued to exist and was even strengthened by the early emperors. Under the Republic it was the citizen who was responsible for proper worship; *peregrini* were only liable for the observance of public morals and orderly conduct. In their nature the problems raised by the imperial and civic religious systems may have been similar, but historically and juristically they were distinct. One was concerned with citizens, the other with devotees of the provincial cult. The effect of Mommsen's hypothesis is to give the new imperial religion a power and influence independent of the civic religion. We may well doubt whether such a view is strictly historical. It certainly destroys the unique importance of *civitas* in Roman public life.

That the crime for which Christians were liable often had something to do with the civic cult is indicated by the fact that they were asked to worship before the statues of the gods as well as before that of the Emperor.[125] Finally, a distinction was usually made between citizens and non-citizens. Pliny, himself, sentenced the non-citizens to death and sent Roman citizens for judgment to Rome.[126] In the trial of the Christians at Lyons, the Roman citizens were decapitated after the approval of the Emperor had been secured, non-citizens were executed in the arena.[127] In view of the fact that the law of *Maiestas* which, according to Mommsen, provided the basis for the charge, abolished all the ordinary distinctions between citizen and non-citizen, it is strange to find traces of *the distinction* in so many instances of the persecution.[128] In the pagan sphere we know of interdicts against Druid rites addressed to *peregrini* after a similar prohibition directed to Roman citizens.[129]

Application of Old or Well Established Rules of Roman Law in the Persecution of Christianity.

The persecution of Christianity was not grounded in any new principle but in old or well established laws. Furthermore, such laws as *Maiestas* and *Sacrilegium* had a much wider application than their terms would imply and could easily be employed against Christians. The evidence of Tertullian in this connection is decisive.[130] He begins his enumeration of the laws which were passed against Christians with the old decree of the Senate forbidding a general to consecrate a god without the permission of the Senate.[131] Besides the various rules dating from the Republican period, there were several imperial laws going back to the beginning of the regime that were invoked against the Christians. Tertullian uses the terms *maiestas* and *sacrilegium*, and despite the efforts of critics to question the correctness of this usage, there is little doubt that the terms did constitute the basis of some charges against the Christians.[132] The sentence pronounced in A.D. 179 on St. Symphorian states, " Maiestatis sacrilegium perpetravit."[133] Constans II applied to counterfeiters not the *Lex Cornelia De Falsis*, but the *Lex Julia De Maiestate*, and found them guilty of sacrilege.[134] We have the testimony of Tacitus, that under Tiberius *maiestas* became the " complementum omnium criminum."[135] Various documents point to such an amalgamation of crimes. A rescript, probably from the time of Tiberius, imposing a penalty for violation of sepulture, appears to assimilate the crime against the dead to the crime against the gods and to make of it a *sacrilegium*. In other words, there was a " rapprochement between the places *sacri*, reserved to superior divinities, and places *religiosi*,

45

those reserved to underworld divinities."[136]   Another document, this time an edict of the Emperor Augustus, dismissing certain charges against several men accused of circulating false rumours about the Emperor but ordering them to be held on a charge of stealing public statues (" and one of these statues bore my name ") shows the close ties existing between *sacrilegium* and *maiestas*, and the extensive application of the latter.[137] The sentence given St. Cyprian indicates how these crimes were attached to the profession of Christianity, " You have lived long years in the spirit of sacrilege ; you have made yourself the chief of a conspiracy ; you have declared yourself the enemy of the gods of Rome and of its sacred laws."[138]   The existence of a crime of lèse-majesté linked to that of lèse-réligion does not rule out two other alternatives ; first, that the several crimes of common law, such as witchcraft and illegal assembly, were at the basis of the persecution ; or second, that the name of Christianity became the object of prosecution.[139]   In defence of the former view may be cited the words employed to describe Christians, *hostis*,[140] *hostis deorum*,[141] *humani generis inimicus*.[142] It is not impossible that some " institutum " of Tiberius, linking crimes against public morality, religion and the state, was invoked against the Christians.[143]   This would have accorded well with the practice under the Republic, as revealed in the Bacchanalian affair.

Whichever view we adopt, there appears without doubt to have been a direct connection between the typical cases of both periods.   In the Imperial as in the Republican period death was often the penalty.[144] In both circumstances the procedure was often *extra ordinem*, that is, conducted within the competence of the magistrate.[145]   The two periods betray a remarkable resemblance in the procedure employed against individuals *in manu* and *in potestate*, as in the typical incidents of the Bacchanalian women and of Pomponia Græcina. The link, however, between the earlier and the later situations cannot be regarded as complete as long as the conviction remains prevalent among students that the religious crime ceased to exist in the late Republic.

VII. The Crime of Lèse Religion—Question of its Existence.

Four points are usually urged against the existence of a religious offence : (*a*) absence of tests ;[146] (*b*) lack of competence of religious tribunals ;[147] (*c*) the theory implied in the words of Tiberius, " that the gods avenge their own wrongs ;[148] (*d*) the apparent absence of trials in cases of suppression.[149] In reference to the first item we may merely state that it is based on an *argumentum ex silentio*. For all we know there may have been precedents for the obligation imposed on citizens in later times to celebrate the anniversary of Cæsar's death.[150]

In regard to the second point one may remark that the civil tribunal had taken over the functions of the religious tribunal. Nevertheless, there is a provision of the *Lex Ursonensis* which gives the Augurs jurisdiction in their own sphere.[151] Was this a slip of the draftsman's pen ?[152] Even if such were the case the fact would indicate that the gap between the older system, when religious officers had jurisdiction, and the new one, when civil officers assumed such jurisdiction, was not great and that in common parlance the religious officials were still regarded as exercising jurisdiction, though really indirectly. The usual arrangement is illustrated by the case of Clodius. When the pontiffs stigmatized the violator of Bona Dea as *nefas*, the case automatically passed into the hands of the consul and the Senate.[153]   This arrangement shows clearly how the religious control over offences that fell within its own sphere had been transferred to the civil officials.

The words of Tiberius will be dealt with presently ; it is to be noted, however, that, if applied, they contravened a fundamental principle of old Roman law : that the community had to expiate the sin of the offender if it did not in some way absolve itself of this guilt.[154]

Irregular Procedure Due to Undeveloped Character.

The apparent absence of a regular trial procedure is a more serious argument against the existence of a crime of *religionsfrevel*.[155]   It must be remembered, however, that the criminal law was comparatively *jejeune* in Rome until the time of Augustus and that as a consequence the religious offence might not have been penalized as a crime in the proper sense of the word.   The place of criminal law was taken in earlier times by the delict or offence against an individual.   The individual, the community in this case, avenged itself on the offending person through its representative, the assembly or the magistrate.[156]   Each such act of vengeance was self-motivated and unconnected with any other.   The act also declared the punishment to be meted out to the offender.   The next great advance in the development of the criminal law was the passage of the *Lex Calpurnia De Repetundis*, which established a standing commission to try cases of extortion and at the same time clearly

48

defined the offences which the commission was competent to try. "It was therefore a regular criminal judicature administering a true criminal jurisprudence."[157] Unfortunately, these permanent commissions were political in their origin and development; they became instruments of power rather than of justice and fell into the hands of factions.[158] Hence they did not serve to gather up all the offences which would have properly fallen within the sphere of a developed criminal law. *Violatio sepulchri*, or the violation of a tomb, for example, remained a sort of private or *botworthy* offence until the time of Augustus, though it appears to have been a real criminal infraction in old Roman law.[159] Even the criminal legislation of Sulla which instituted a new arrangement of the *quæstiones*, and the reforming legislation of Augustus did not entirely eliminate the scope of private redress, for soon thereafter the law began to take account of a new type of crime called *crimen extraordinarium*, indicating that the regular classification of crime was not keeping pace with the moral development of the community which insisted on regarding many other offences than those specified by the law as crimes.[160]

One of the offences which was probably never properly co-ordinated was the religious crime. The delictual nature of the offence is implicit in the trials of the Bacchanalian women and of Pomponia Græcina. In other cases, it is evidenced by the absence of any action at all on the part of the government. We have said that the religious crime articulated imperfectly with the criminal law because we are of the opinion that though not defined outright, the *crimen laesae religionis* was so linked with other offences as to have been unmistakable. This linking of crimes, sometimes widely different in character, under one rubric, was common in Roman law and was a result of the nature of the statute creating the *quaestio* which was itself called forth by temporary exigencies. Perjury was in this way linked with poisoning because the *Lex Cornelia de Sicariis et Veneficis* had " given jurisdiction over these forms of crime to the same permanent commission."[161] Even when the classification was not so capricious the name of one crime was often applied to that of another which was only superficially similar to it. Such was the fate of *sacrilegium* and *quasi-sacrilegium*, which, though originally denoting the crime of theft from a temple came to include such crimes as *sepulchri violatio* and of *religionsfrevel*.[162]

The religious crime was also probably linked with immorality and treason, but it is difficult to say with exactitude by what term it was described, *malum carnem* or *crimen laesae religionis*. Whatever the legal instruments which put it into effect, we may feel confident that we are informed on the nature of the offence it defined : the practice of *sacra externa*.[163]

When we take up the subject of penalties imposed for violation of the law we must also realize the primitive character of the society in which the religious sin was first defined. The earliest *religionsfrevel* probably brought down on the head of the guilty one the sentence of *devotio*, or of *sacratio*, involved in the words *sacer esto*.[164] That is, the person whose guilt threatened to pollute the community was outlawed and it became every man's right or duty to strike him down.[165] Eventually the magistrates by means of an action of *perduellio*, took over the task, but in early times the victim was, as it were, turned over to the gods for punishment which, when it came, even at the hands of man, was regarded as the act of the deity.[166]

It is in this sense that the words of Tiberius cited above should be understood ; not in the sense of letting the culprit get off scot free. If it is objected that the " culprit will do precisely that if no one strikes him down," and that we therefore have no crime properly speaking involved in the sentence of *sacratio*, we may agree, with the understanding, however, that there was a time when even political offences were not regarded as crimes. There appears to be no doubt that the *sacratio* pronounced on the violator of the tribune was of this sort and, if the worst penalty which the means at the disposal of a whole class could ensure were no more severe it is not strange to find the religious offence penalized with similar leniency.[167] Of course, not all religious infractions entailed *sacratio* ; the milder offences brought fines (*multae*) or expiratory offerings, (*piacula*).[168]

If we recall that the history of torts and sins precedes that of crime, that crime appears first as a *privilegium*, and that even after the establishment of a regular criminal law a great many offences still remain delicts or imperfectly defined crimes, we may understand the absence of a regular judicature and trial procedure in cases in which the community had to punish offenders against the state religion.

Supposed Breakdowns of Roman Religion.

The disappearance of the religious crime is often coupled with a supposed breakdown in Roman religion in the last days of the Republic.[169] We may well question on grounds of historical continuity a breakdown in religion and morality in any age. The complaints which one encounters on this score in the Latin writers are really complaints against progress in a society which was based on the dogma of changelessness.[170] One may be led astray by the *De Natura Deorum* of Cicero into picturing the society of his time as utterly sceptical and irreligious. According to Augustine the pontiff Scaevola wished to distinguish the religion of the citizen ("religio civilis") from that of the poets.[171] He might have urged a similar caution against censorious moralists who, like Tacitus, insisted on finding religion and society involved in common ruin. For the age of Cicero the evidence on the religious situation has been examined by several students with the conclusion that the theory of a breakdown of religion is a gross exaggeration.[172] Indeed, if we judge from the Augustan restoration, we are dealing in this period with a new and deep religious feeling.[173] Evidence for the Antonine Age, presented by Dill, seems to lead to the same conclusion for that period.[174] Epigraphic data attest the survival of the cult of the *di indigetes* throughout the Empire.[175] The results of all these investigations testify to the conservatism, and the keen sense of religious contract characteristic of the Romans to the latest days. There is nothing in the evidence to denote the disappearance of the religio-civic bond.

VIII. *Conclusion : Application to Judaism.*

Whatever answer we give to the question of the existence of a *crimen laesae religionis*, or religious crime, nevertheless the two principles with which we have attempted to link such a crime appear to be beyond dispute. Roman citizenship was exclusive. The practise of foreign national rites if unauthorized by the government was forbidden.

It remains to ask how Judaism could have been professed by Roman citizens if it were a foreign national religion, as Juster and Mommsen maintain. Juster has invoked the inevitable hypothesis to explain the difficulty. " The tolerance of these customs and the privileges that it entailed would, according to Roman principles, have applied only to Jewish *peregrini* (foreigners) and not to Jewish citizens of Rome. However, by a special favour, the latter were permitted to share the privileges of Jewish *peregrini*."[176]

We may well feel dubious, however, about the existence of a " favour " or privilege that would have struck at the very basis of an important chapter in Roman Public Law.

NOTES

[1] Unlike the system in most Greek cities.

[2] Cicero, *Pro Balbo*, 11 ; *Pro Caecina*, 33 and 34 ; *De Oratore*, I, 40 ; *Pro Domo*, 29, 30.

[3] Nepos, *Atticus*, 3.

[4] Gaius, I, 131.

[5] *Pro Balbo*, 11, 28.

[6] *Atticus*, 3.

[7] Gaius, I, 131.

[8] J. Anderson in *Journal of Roman Studies*, 1929, p. 221.

[9] Mommsen, *Römisches Staatsrecht*, Leipzig, 1887, (3 auflage), 3 band, 1 abt., p. 47.

[10] *Op. cit.*, p. 47-48.

[11] *Cuq*, article " Origo," *Dict. des. ant. gr. et rom.*

[12] E. G. Hardy, *Roman Laws and Charters*, 133, asserts that what prevented the Gallic nobles from being admitted to the Senate under Claudius was the lack of a " Municipalis Origo." H. J. Cunningham, *Classical Quarterly*, 1914, pp. 132 to 133, 1915, pp. 56 to 60, denies that the terms " coloniae " and " municipae " used by Claudius have such a connotation.

[13] Cuq. *loc. cit.*, p. 237.

[14] J. Declareuil, *Rome The Law Giver*, New York, tr., 1926, 54. Cicero, *De Legibus*, 2, 1. *Digest*, 50, 1, 1 to 2, 6. Examples were, the freedman of two patrons whose *origines* differed, and the person adrogated who retained his own *origo* while acquiring that of the adrogator.

[15] V. Chapot, *Le Monde romain*, pp. 119–120. Cf. S. Dill, *Roman Society From Nero to Marcus Aurelius*, London, 1920, p. 244, " a resident alien (incola) or an augustal might be coöpted into the splendid order of the Curia or he might be allowed to wear its badges or those of some office which he could not actually hold."

[16] Mommsen, *op. cit.*, p. 48.

[17] *Ibid.*

[18] Hartmann, *De Exilio Apud Romanos*, pp. 2 ff. Humbert, article " Exilium," *Dict. des ant. gr. et rom.*, vol. 2, part 1, p. 943.—F. Baudry, article " Caput," *loc. cit.*, vol. 1, part 2, p. 912.—Mommsen, *Röm. Straf.*, p. 65 ff.

[19] Polybius, VI, 14, 7.

[20] Mommsen, *Röm. Strafrecht*, pp. 68–69.—Strachan-Davidson, *Problems of the Roman Criminal Law*, II, 53.

[21] Sallust, *Cat.*, 51, 22. " Aliae leges condemnatis civibus non animam eripi sed exilium permitti jubent."—Cicero, *Pro Caecina*, 34, 100; *De Domo*, 30, 78.—A. Gasquy, *Cicéron jurisconsulte*, Paris, 1887, p. 250.—Strachan-Davidson, *op. cit.*, II, pp. 26 to 27.

[22] Mommsen urges two facts in proof of the view that from Sulla to Tiberius, a Roman, condemned and *relegatus*, retained his citizenship. The first is that *Oppianicius*, whose father was convicted on a charge of poisoning, owned one

of his father's slaves. (*Cicero, Pro Cluentio*, 63, 176). " The
elder Oppianicius must therefore have had the right of
bequeathing property and have been a Roman citizen."
The second fact Mommsen finds in the *Lex Julia Municipalis*,
(verse 118), which disqualifies for municipal office anyone
condemned on a capital charge, thus implying that such
condemnation did not involve loss of citizenship. Both
these facts are successfully explained by Strachan-Davidson,
op. cit., II, pp. 70–71. Cicero would not try so hard to
prove that he never lost his citizenship unless it were well
known that such was the usual result of citizens going into
exile. *Ad Herennium*, II, 28, 45.

(23) Cicero, *Ad Atticum*, X, 8, 2.

(24) Cicero, *De Haruspicum Responsis*, 8, 17.

(25) Cicero, *Ad Atticum*, X, 14, 3.

(26) Dio Cassius, LVII, 22, 5: "In A.D. 23 Tiberius denied to those
who were interdicted from fire and water the right to make
a will." Strachan-Davidson, *op. cit.*, II, 56.

(27) Ovid, *Tristia*, V, 11, 9. . . .
Nec vitam nec opes nec ius mihi civis ademit
Nil nisi me partriis iussit abesse facis.
Ipse relegati non exulis utitur in me
Nomine.

(28) Strachan-Davidson, *op. cit.*, II, p. 67.

(29) The area out of which a convict Roman citizen or former
convict citizen was warned kept growing in extent until,
after the Social war, it included all of Italy. Moreover, the
federate states in which assumption of citizenship automatically cancelled the Roman citizenship of the exile, by
virtue of certain treaty agreements, were mostly situated in
Italy and were thus eliminated from the territory to which
a Roman citizen under condemnation might have recourse.
The whole process here parallels the development that was
going on in the whole notion of citizenship, as we have
pointed out. See Strachan-Davidson, *op. cit.*, II, p. 37.

(30) H. J. Rose, ed., *Roman Questions of Plutarch*, Oxford, 1924, p. 85.

[31] Cicero, *De Nat. Deorum*, II, 2 ; *De Har. Resp.*, 9.

[32] *Dio Cassius*, LIII, 2.

[33] J. B. Carter, *Religious Life of Ancient Rome*, Boston, 1911, p. 25. On Etruscan influence, see L. Homo, *Primitive Italy and the Beginnings of Roman Imperialism*, New York, 1926, p. 12.

[34] Carter, *op. cit.*, pp. 25–27. On the *pomoerium* within which the gods of the state might be worshipped, see Varro, *Lingua Latina*, V, 143. See below.

[35] Boissier, *La Religion romaine*, I, 39.

[36] Giessen Papyrus, P. M. Meyer, *Juristische Papyri*, Berlin, 1920, no. 1. The text is based on a possible reading of this difficult papyrus, based on the article by J. Stroux in *Philologus* (Leipzig), LXXXVIII, 1933, p. 272.

[37] Cf. terms like *supplicum* from *sub placeo* involving the notion of death as a sin offering and *castigatio* from *castum agere* involving the notion of purification through atonement.

[38] A. H. J. Greenidge, *Roman Public Life*, London, 1922, p. 51.

[39] *Ibid.*

[40] L. Mitteis, *Romisches Privatrecht*, p. 26, finds little trace of the influence of *fas* in the law of property as relating to living persons. The presence of *fas* in the law of family and inheritance is explained by the fact that marriage was regarded as *divini humanique iuris communicatio*. Modestinus in *Digest*, XXIII, II, 1. See G. Wissowa, art. " Law (Roman)," Hastings' *Encyclopedia of Religion and Ethics*, vol VII, p. 884.

[41] Livy, I, 20, " ne quid divini iuris negligendo patrios ritus peregrinosque adsciscendo, turbaretur."

[42] Livy, I, 20, " Numa cetera quoque omnia publica privataque sacra pontificis scitis subiecit." Greenidge, *op. cit.*, p. 51.

([43]) Livy, X, 7, "deorum magis quam nostra causa expetimus ut quos privatim colimus publice colamus." (The words of the consul Decius).

([44]) E. Merrill in *Classical Journal*, XV, 196 to 215.

([45]) A. Grenier, *The Roman Spirit*, New York, 1926, p. 92. Wissowa, *Religion and Kultus*, p. 113.

([46]) J. B. Carter, *Religious Life of Ancient Rome*, p. 41. Wissowa, *op. cit.*, p. 250.

([47]) Wissowa, *op. cit.*, p. 263.—H. Graillot, *Le Culte de Cybèle, Mère des Dieux à Rome et dans l'empire romain*, Paris, 1912.

([48]) Carter, *op. cit.*, p. 42. . . . Wissowa, *op. cit.*, p. 253.

([49]) Tertullian, *Apologeticus*, V, 1.—Arnobius, *Adversus Gentes*, II, 73.

([50]) Livy, IV, 46: "Ne quis templum aramne iniussu Senatus dedicaret." Tertullian, *Apol.*, VI: "Vetus erat decretum ne quis deus ab imperatore consecraretur, nisi a senatu probatus." *Apol.* XIII, 3: "Status dei cuiusque in senatus aestimatione pendebat." Tertullian, *Ad. Nation.*, I, 10: "Ut deus non sit nisi eum esse permiserit senatus." Aulus Gellius, XIV, 7: "De rebus divinis priusquam humanis ad senatum referendum esse."

([51]) Arnobius, III, 38. The pronunciation Novensides was probably Sabine. See Varro, *Ling. Lat.*, V, 10, 74, according to whom most of the new gods were Sabine.—Wissowa, *Religion und Kultus*, p. 91, 198, 239. *Di Novensiles* might gain access within the *pomoerium* if identified with certain of the *Di indigetes*. Cybele was in this way identified with the Roman Magna Mater. This tendency to identify new gods with old ones reveals the chauvinistic character of this syncretism. Demeter, Dionysos, and Kore entered Rome in the guise of the old Roman deities, Ceres, Liber, and Libera. J. B. Carter, *op. cit.*, p. 40. The worship of Hermes under the new name of Mercury was due to the influence of the Sibylline Oracles. The cult of Hercules, which has been regarded as Greek, was probably Roman. See J. Toutain in *Revue des études latines*, VII, 1928, pp. 200–212.

(52) M. Besnier, art. "Pomoerium," *Dict. des ant. gr. et rom.*, vol. IV, p. 544, according to whom the distinction was between foreign gods from Greece and those of Italy.

(53) According to E. Bickel, *Philologische Wochenschrift*, 1921, pp. 832 to 838, the antithesis is between gods and deified heroes.—Wissowa, in *Hermes*, 1921, 113 to 130, denies that Varro's classification had any official basis.

(54) Besnier, *loc. cit.*, p. 544.

(55) Pomponius in *Digest*, XII, 7, 36 (passage cited in introduction). Cf. *Digest*, XLVII, 12, 4, " sepulcra hostium nobis religiosa non sunt."

(56) H. J. Rose, in *Classical Quarterly*, XXIV, 1930, pp. 129 to 135.

(57) Boissier, *La Religion romaine*, I, 347 to 348.

(58) Cicero, *De Legibus*, II, 8. Separatim nemo habessit deos ; neve novos sive advenas, nisi publice adscitos, privatim colunto.—On whether Cicero records an old penal law imposing a capital sentence see P. Vigneaux, *Etude sur l'histoire de la Praefectura Urbis à Rome*, Paris, 1896, p. 208.

(59) *De Legibus*, II, 12.

(60) Livy, XXV, 1 : " M. Aemilio praetori urbis negotium ab senatu datum est, ut eis religionibus populum liberaret . . . et edixit ut . . . ne quis in publico sacrove loco novo aut externo ritu sacrificaret." The author translates *religionibus* as rites rather than " scruples," which is the usual meaning of the term.

(61) Livy, I, 20 (passage cited above) : " Omnia publica privataque sacra pontificis scitis subiecit."

(62) Dio Cassius, 52, 36.

(63) Mommsen, *Röm. Strafrecht*, pp. 555, 567 ff.

(64) Aurel. Vict., *De Ill. Vir.*, 72 ; Val. Max., IV, 4, 11. Sallust *Jug.*, 15, 25, 28, 29, 40 ; Plutarch, *Quaest. Rom.*, c, 50, Ascon.

in Scaur, pp. 21, 22 ; Cicero, *Brutus*, 29, 30, 35 ; *De Orat.*, 1, 49 ; *Pro Mur.*, 17 : " Quod eius opera sacra multa populi Romani deminuta esse diceret ; crimini dabat sacra publica populi R. deum penatium quae Lavini fierent opera eius minus recte casteque fieri."

[65] Paul, *Senten.*, 5, 21, 2 : " Qui novas sectas vel ratione incognitas religiones inducunt ex quibus animi hominum moveantur, honestiores deportantur, humiliores capite puniuntur." Compare Servius in *Aen.*, VIII, 187 : " Cautum fuerat ne quis novas introduceret religiones."

[66] Modestinus in *Digest*, 48, 19, 30, " si quis aliquid fecerit quo leves hominum animi superstitione numinis terrerentur divus Marcus huiusmodi homines in insulam relegari rescripsit."

[67] Pallu De Lessert, *Bulletin de la Société Nationale des Antiquaires de France*, 1916, p. 113. F. Martroye, *loc. cit.*, p. 111, points out that in Plautus, Cicero, Ennius, the word means conjurer or sorcerer.

[68] F. Martroye, *loc. cit.*, p. 106. In the Constitutions of Theodosius the word is applied to Jews and heretics.

[69] E. Cuq., *Mélanges d'archéologie et d'histoire*, (*Ecole Francaise de Rome*), VI, 1886, pp. 114 to 138. It was not unusual for terms like *malum carmen* to have a general import which applied equally to different offences of the criminal law. The analogy of such a term as *nexum* which underwent specialization is instructive. See below.

[70] Cicero, II, 10, 25. " Suosque deos aut. novos aut alienigenas coli confusionem habet religionum et ignotas ceremonias sacerdotibus."

[71] The question whether Cicero's two works, the *De Republica* and the *De Legibus* were wholly theoretical has come to be answered in the negative. For the general question, see E. Meyer, *Caesar's Monarchie*, Berlin, 1920, and R. Heinze, in *Hermes*, LIX, 1924, p. 77.

[72] Dionysius II, 19. *Roman Antiquities*, tr. E. Spelman, London, 1758.

[73] C. I. L., VI, 2182. Cf. large number of other instances in inscriptions of Roman citizens belonging to "foreign" (but authorized) cults.

[74] E. G. Hardy, *Christianity and the Roman Government*, London, 1894, pp. 9–10.

[75] C. Callewaert in *Revue des Questions historiques*, 1907, t. LXXXII, p. 17, 19, affirms it rather cautiously : " N'est-il pas permis d'aller plus loin et de considérer au moins quelquesunes de ces mesures comme de vrais lois pénales. Que faut-il de plus, à l'époque de la décadence, pour avoir de véritables lois criminelles qu'on peut invoquer au moins devant les juges statuant *extra ordinem* ? "

[76] Bentham's *Fragment on Government* and Austin's *Province of Jurisprudence Determined*, divide each law into a command of the legislator, an obligation imposed on the individual, and a sanction for breach of command. This, however, is characteristic only of mature jurisprudence, as Maine points out. *Ancient Law*, p. 4.

[77] Mommsen, *Rom. Straf.*, p. 567–570, 578–580. *Idem*, " Der Religionsfrevel nach römischen Recht," in *Hist. Zeitschrift*, 1890, t. LXIV, p. 392, 393.—P. F. Girard, *Organisations judiciaires des Romains*, Paris, 1901, p. 55.—G. Wissowa, article, " Vestalinnenfrevel " in *Archiv fur Religionswissenschaft*, 1923, 201–215.

[78] Mommsen, *Hist. Zeit.*, *ibid.* Girard, *loc. cit.* : " Cette séparation devait amener a sa suite l'impunité des délits contre les dieux par cette simple raison que ceux qui avaient le droit de punir n'avaient plus a s'occuper des choses divines et que ceux qui s'occupaient des choses divines n'avaient plus le droit de punir."

[79] Mommsen, *Röm. Straf.*, pp. 568, 579—" the old laws appeared to take no account of lack of faith."

[80] A. D. Drachman, *Atheism in Pagan Antiquity*, Copenhagen, 1922, p. 8.

[81] Lipsius, *Das Attische Recht und Rechtverfahren*, I, p. 358.

(82) Drachman, *op. cit.*, p. 6, who asserts that the sentences were illegal.

(83) Tacitus, *Annales*, I, 73, cf. Tertullian *Apologet.*, ch. XXVIII: "Ne prae manu esset jure libertatis dicere: Nolo mihi Jovem propitium? tu qui es? Me conveniat Janus iratus ex qua velit fronte; qui tibi mecum est?"

(84) Mommsen, *Röm. Straf.*, p. 578 and note 4.

(85) *Op. cit.*, pp. 575, 578. The religious crime, however, was included in the crime of lèse-majesté, rather than under a separate head. Did it spring from the incompatibility between monotheism and the divinity of the Emperor? *Op. cit.*, p. 575: "It is therefore logical to consider and to punish as an avowal of lèse-majesté, the declaration made before the tribunal that one adheres to Christianity."

(86) Mommsen himself distinguishes the two, *op. cit.*, p. 570, 571, note: "When one speaks of the apostasy of the non-citizen, there is no reference to the abandonment of the religion of the city but to the abandonment of the religion of the Empire."

(87) Livy, IV, 30: "Donec publicus iam pudor ad primores civitatis pervenit cernentes in omnibus vicis sacellisque peregrina atque insolita piacula pacis deum exposcendae."

(88) Livy, XXV, 1, passage cited above.

(89) Livy, XXXIX, 16.

(90) Wissowa, *Religion und Kultus der Romer*, p. 57, 58. Cicero, *De Legibus*, II, 15.

(91) Waltzing, *Les Corporations professionelles chez les romains*, 4 vols., Paris, 1895–1900, I, 79. Porcius Latro cites an old Gabinian Law: "Lege Gabinia promulgatum qui coitiones ullas clandestinas in urbe conflavisset more majorum capitali supplicio multaretur." Cf. Ulpian in *Digest*, I (*De Colleg. et corpor.*, XLVII, 22): "Quisquis illicitum collegium usurpaverit sua poena tenetur qua tenentur qui hominibus armatis loca publica vel templa occupasse judicati sunt."

(92) Cuq. in *Mélanges d'archéologie et d'histoire*, 1886, t. VI, pp. 114–138, according to whom the term " odium " employed by Tacitus of the Christians was a real charge going back to the Twelve Tables and associated with the crime of practising magic.

(93) H. Bernard, *Le Senatus Consulte des Bacchanales*, Paris, 1908, pp. 119–120, 129.

(94) F. Lenormant, art. " Bachanalia," *Dict. des ant. gr. et rom.*, t. I, p. 590. *Idem, La Grande Grèce*, t. I, p. 422.

In both works the author emphasizes the baneful Etruscan influence. See also Wissowa in Pauly, *Real Encyclopädie*, art. " Dionysos." Bernard, *op. cit.*, p. 32 cites probable practice of human sacrifices. Livy himself says, " pro victimis immolari." Livy, XXXIX, 13.

(95) Cf. the provisions of the Senatus Consultum in *C. I. L.*, no. 196; in Bernard, *op. cit.*, pp. 51–52 : " Homines plus voinvorsi viri atque mulieres sacra ne quisquam fecise velet, neve interibei virei plus duobus, mulieribus plus tribus arfuise velent, nisi de pr(aitoris) urbani senatusque sententia utei suprad scriptum est." Besides this provision, permitting a small number of votaries to celebrate the cult, we have epigraphic evidence that the cult continued to exist even though " Etruscan painted vases which had borrowed imagery of the cult no longer carry the motifs." Bernard, *op. cit.*, and C. I. G. 5762. Cf. also Mommsen, *Inscriptiones regni Neapolitani*, 2477. Cf. Conclusion of Bernard, p. 75 : " Le Culte de Bacchus, en principe, ne fut pas prohibé."

(96) Within the limits described, no distinction was made between public and private practice. See S. C. in Bernard, *op. cit.*, p. 52, " neve in poplicod neve in preivatod neve extrad urbem sacra quisquam fecisse velet—nisi pr(aitorem) urbanum adieset, isque de senatuos sententiad dum ne minus senatoribus C. Adesent quom ea res cosoleretur, jousiset."

(97) " Bacas vir nequis adiese velet civis Romanus neve nominus Latini neve socium quisquam." The view that citizens were lumped with *peregrini* because their complicity had deprived

them of citizenship (which echoes Cicero's theory in the Catilinarian Orations), is espoused by Mommsen, *Röm. Staatsrecht*, and Bernard, *op. cit.*, p. 94. Willems, *Le Sénat de la République*, II, p. 285, on the other hand regards the whole affair as judicial, and the senatorial commissions in Apulia and Sardinia as mere investigating bodies rather than *quaestiones extraordinariae*, exercising a criminal jurisdiction. Strachan-Davidson, *Problems of Roman Criminal Law*, I, p. 235, also regards the affair as essentially judicial, and the powers exercised as a " resurrection of the full magisterial *imperium*."

[98] S. Reinach in *Revue archéologique*, 1908, pp. 236–253, who regards the official charges as mere pretexts for the pursuit of political conspiracy.

[99] *Ibid.*

[100] For discussion, see Strachan-Davidson, *Problems of Roman Criminal Law*, I, 232–245.

[101] Paul, *Sentent*, V, XXIX, 2 : " Cum de eo quaeritur nulla dignitas a tormentis excipitur." Cf. also Ammianus Marcellinus L., XXIX, C. XII : "Ubi majestas pulsata defenditur a quaestionibus vel cruentis nullam corneliae leges exemere fortunam."

[102] Cf. Bernard, *Senatus Consulte*, p. 58 : " Si ques esent qui avorsum ead fecisent eeis rem caputalem faciendam censuere."

[103] Livy, XXXIX, 18, 6. Tacitus, *Ann.* 13, 32. See below.

[103a] Valerius Maximus, I, III, 2, as extracted by Nepotianus : " *Idem* (praetor Hispalus) Judaeos qui Sabazii Jovis cultu simulato mores Romanos inficere conati sunt domos suas repetere coegit."

[104] F. Cumont, *Comptes rendus de l'Académie des Inscriptions*, 1906, p. 63–79. A. Jamar, *Musée Belge*, 1909, t. XIII, p. 227–252.

[105] H. Gressman in *Jewish Studies in Memory of Israel Abrahams* New York, 1927, pp. 170 ff. Sabazius came from Phrygia and was known as Hypsistos. He was often linked with

Hermes and with Mercury, who is called the "divine angel" in Phrygian inscriptions. In Apamea there had existed from early times a Jewish community which, according to the Talmud, had forsaken Jerusalem and which exercised great influence, as is evidenced in coins of the period of Philip the Arab depicting Noah's Ark landing in Apamea. The tomb of Vincentius (A.D. 250) reveals a curious mingling of Jewish and Sabazian influences. On the basis of such facts Gressman vindicates the probability of an expulsion of Jewish-Sabazian sectaries in 139 B.C.

(106) The expulsions of foreigners from Rome can, of course, be traced to a variety of causes depending on circumstances. R. W. Husband, "Expulsions of Foreigners from Rome." *Classical Philology*, 1916, 315–333. Under the Republic, for example, foreigners who had surreptitiously assumed the name of Roman citizens and in that way usurped political privileges, opened themselves often, but not always, to criminal prosecution. Archias, for example, was prosecuted on the basis of a law passed by Gaius Papius (65 B.C.). However, a criminal prosecution was not always undertaken. Livy, XXXIX, 3, tells us that in 187 B.C. delegates came from the Italian towns to complain of large numbers of their residents moving to Rome. The Senate in reply issued an edict expelling these strangers, but imposed no penalties. In 177 B.C. the Senate, now realizing the futility of dealing peaceably with the problem, empowered the praetor to use his *ius coercitionis* to expel foreigners. Nevertheless, in the instance cited by Valerius Maximus, religious motives were obviously at work.

(107) Tacitus, *Ann.*, 13, 32: "Et Pomponia Graecina insignis femina, a Plautio, quem ovasse de Britannis rettuli, nupta ac superstitionis externae rea, mariti iudicio permissa; isque prisco instituto propinquis coram de capite famaque coniugis cognovit et insontem nuntiavit."

(108) For the view that the charge was adultery see the note in Furneaux's edition of the *Annales*, II, p. 195, who compares it with the case of the Bacchanal women. In neither case, however, do our texts support such an hypothesis. Cf. Nipperdey and Lightfoot, *St. Clement*, London, 1890, I, 30.

64

Adultery was simply one of the crimes of which the household tribunal took cognizance. Tacitus *Ann.* II, 50, 5 : " Adulterii graviorem poenam deprecatus ut exemplo majorum propinquis suis ultra ducentesimum lapidem removeretur suasit."

(109) De Rossi, *Roma Sotteranea Christiana*, Rome, 1863–1867, II, 360–364.

(110) Mommsen, *Röm. Str.*, p. 18 ff., would seem to imply that the *tutela gentilium* which represented rights over the woman's person and property in the absence of either father or husband was the equivalent of the *manus*. Girard also, *Org. jud.*, p. 97, note 1, describes the tutor as possessing a *potestas* over the woman. It is difficult to see how the state could have countenanced such a system of private jurisdiction in later times. Livy, XXXIX, 18, 6, distinguishes in connection with the Bacchanalian affair between women who were subject to the household jurisdiction (in manu) and those not so subject (sui juris). Yet there is the instance of Publilia and Licinia, who were accused of poisoning their husbands before the ordinary courts but were put to death by their *propinqui* before the court could act. Strachan-Davidson, *op. cit.*, I, 35, believes that they were in the *potestas* of their fathers and had never passed into the *manus* of their husbands. There appears little doubt that women *in manu* always remained subject to the household jurisdiction ; there is some doubt about women *sui juris*. Here we have strong presumptive evidence of the undeveloped character of criminal jurisprudence in Rome up to a late date. For Publilia and Licinia, see Livy, *Epitome*, 48, and Valerius Maximus, VI, 3, 8.

(111) Mommsen, *Röm. Str.*, p. 18.

(112) See chapters five and six of present work.

(113) Dio Cassius in *Epitome of Xiphilinus*, LXVII, 14 (cf. also Suetonius, *Dom.*, 15): " The same year Domitian caused to die several people, among others the consul, Flavius Clemens, although this was his cousin and had married one of his nieces, Flavia Domitilla. Both of them were accused

of atheism, an accusation which condemned many others convicted of having submitted to Jewish customs. Some were put to death, others punished with confiscation. As for Domitilla, she was only exiled to Pandataria." The significance of this passage for the Jewish question will be taken up below. Were Flavius and Domitilla Christians ? This seems likely in the case of the latter. See articles by Leclercq, " Domitien," and " Domitille (Cimetiere de)," *Dict. d'arch. chrét.*, Fasc. XL.

(114) *Röm. Str.*, p. 572, note 2, p. 575. The criticism is made of Tertullian's use of the word in the expression " sacrilegii et majestatis rei convenimur," *Apol.*, ch. 10.

(115) See below.

(116) H. Delehaye, " La persécution dans l'armee sous Diolétian," *Bulletin de la classe des lettres de l'Académie royale de Belgique*, 1921, 150–166, points out that the persecutions under Diocletian resulted in the elimination of a large number of officers from the army, but in very few cases of martyrdom. It was undoubtedly true that those in public life or holding public office were more subject to annoyance than private individuals, but, in general, persecution was not severe. It did become severe as Paribeni points out, *Cristianesimo e impero, Rendiconti della r. academia dei Lincei*, III, 13, 1927, 684–697, under certain Emperors, who conceived of Christianity as a political menace. The feeling which Christianity inspired in people, according to Paribeni, was akin to that felt by some people in our own day toward Bolshevism.

(117) Three main systems have been proposed to explain the persecution of Christianity prior to about A.D. 202, that of persecution by the *ius coercitionis*, developed by Mommsen in the article cited in *Hist. Zeits.*, 1890, 389–425, that of persecution by ordinary criminal laws, expressed in Le Blant's *Bases juridiques des poursuites*, and the theory of a law of exception striking at Christians directly, defended with great skill by C. Callewaert in *Revue d'histoire ecclesiastique*, 1901, p. 771–797; 1902, p. 5–15, 324–348, 601–614; in *Revue des Questions Historiques*, 1903, p. 28–55.—It is our

purpose to defend the view of a continuity in the Roman theory of *religionsfrevel* on grounds common to all these systems, but to avoid extended discussion of the *instument* of Roman policy. For a summary of the question, cf. H. Leclercq, article " Droit persécuteur," *Dict. d'arch. chrét, et de lit., fasc.*, XL, cols. 1565–1640.

(118) The examination of the testimony in *Acts* has been performed by Callewaert in *Revue des questions historiques*, 1904, t. LXXVI, pp. 13–14. When, for example, Paul was charged before Festus with violation of the laws of the Jews and of Caesar (*Acts*, XXV, 8), the latter charge apparently had so little foundation that the governor dismissed it. So in all cases, at Corinth (*Acts*, XVIII, 13), and at Philippi (XVI, 20), where Paul, together with the accusers, received stripes.

(119) Bouché-Leclercq, *L'Intolérance réligieuse et la politique*, p. XI, cites the measures of Domitian against Jewish proselytism. See I. Levi, " Le proselytisme juif," *Revue des études juives*, 1907, 5, LIII, pp. 59–61.

(120) As we hope to demonstrate, Judaism was non-national in parts of the Roman world. Two thirds of a total Jewish population of about seven million lived outside Palestine. One should also not forget the non-national influence of the Hellenistic Judaism in this period, as revealed in such a group as the Covenanters of Damascus. Charles, *Apocrypha and Pseudepigrapha of the Old Testament*, 2 vols., Oxford, 1912. See Leclercq in *Dict. d'arch. chrét.* Fasc., LXXX, cols. 90–91, 110–119.

(121) G. F. Moore, *Judaism in the First Centuries*, III, 17, opposing R. H. Charles, *Apocrypha and Pseudepigrapha*, II, p. 69, and Bousset, *Religion des Judenthums in Hellenistischer Zeitalter*, Ed. H. Gressman, Tübingen, 1926, who regard Judaism, after A.D. 70, particularly, as a legalistic sect.

(122) Cf. Travers Herford, *Pharisaism : Its Aim and its Method*, London, 1912, and the evidence collected by Claude G. Montefiore, *The Synoptic Gospels and Rabbinic Literature*, London, 1928. Cf. the same author's chapter in Foakes-Jackson and Lake, *The Beginnings of Christianity*, 3 vols., London, 1920–1931, vol. 1.

[122] *Acts*, XVIII, 12 to 15.

[124] For a study of the Asiatic origin of the provincial cult and its various centres of worship (Pergamum, Three Gauls, Ara Ubiorum), see H. Dieckmann, *Stimmen der Zeit*, XLIX, p. 129–137. For the cult under Tiberius, see Rostovtzef, in *Rev. hist.*, CLXIII, 1930, pp. 1–27.

[125] Beurlier, *Le Culte impérial*, p. 273, opposing Neumann, *Die Römische Staat und die allgemeine Kirche bis auf Diocletian*, Leipzig, 1890, p. 12, who makes the crime of sacrilege depend on the refusal to worship at the Imperial altar. Both Pliny and Trajan show no preference for the Emperor's statue over those of the gods. Leclercq, " Droit perséc.", *Dict. d'arch. chrét.*, fasc., XL, col. 1578.

[126] Pliny, *Ep.*, 96.

[127] Eusebius, 5, 1, 47. Mommsen, *Röm. Str.*, p. 576, note 2.

[128] See note 104 above. Compare the fate of the praetor Gallius whose high office did not spare him the torments usually reserved for slaves. Suetonius, *Octavius*, C. XXVII.

[129] Suetonius, *Claudius*, 25 : " Druidarum religionem apud Gallos dirae immanitatis, et tantum civibus sub Augusto interdictam penitus abolevit."

[130] Tertullian's testimony, as that of a jurist, is of great weight. In consequence every polemicist has sought to find in his writings justification for his own view. Leclercq, " Droit perséc.", *Dict. d'arch. chrét.*, col. 1602.—P. de Labriolle, " Le Droit romain dans l'oeuvre de Tertullien," *Revue des cours et conférences*, 1906, t. XIV, pp. 125–143.

[131] Tertullian, *Apologet.*, V, i : " Ut de origine aliquid retractemus eiusmodi legum vetus erat decretum ne qui deus ab imperatore consecraretur nisi a senatu probatus."

[132] Tertullian, *Apol.*, C. 24 : " Crimen laesae Romanae religionis : inreligiositatis elogium." C. 27, " intentatio laesae divinitatis." C. 28, " ventum est ad secundum titulum laesae

augustioris majestatis." C. 10, "sacrilegii et majestatis rei convenimur."—Mommsen accepts the correctness of the use of *maiestas* by Tertullian, but questions the use of *sacrilegium*. Mommsen, *Röm. Str.*, p. 569, note 2 :—both these crimes required some acts on the part of the accused to render them applicable, such as theft from a temple or destruction of the images of the gods. Tertullian himself says, as if in answer to the charge, " non quos sacrilegos existimatis nec in furto nunquam deprehendistis : nunquam in sacrilegio." Tertul. *Ad Scapul.*, 11. In other words, according to these critics, Tertullian was using these words in their popular rather than legal sense. See Leclercq, " Droit perséc.", *Dict. d'arch. chrét.*, cols., 1575, 76, 77, 78, and C. Callewaert, " Les premiers Chrétiens et l'accusation de lèse-majesté," *Revue des quest. hist.*, 1904, LXXVI, p. 5–28. We are of the opinion that these terms had a legal sense.

(133) Ruinart, *Acta Sincera Martyrum*, ed. Ratisbonne, 1859, p. 127. —E. Cuq., art. " Sacrilegium," in *Dict. des ant. gr. et rom.*, IV, p. 985.

(134) *Cod. Theod.*, IX, 23, 1 : IX, 21, 5 : IX, 38, 6.—Cuq., *loc. cit.*

(135) Tacitus, *Annales*, I, III, 28.

(136) F. Cumont, *Revue historique*, t. CXLIII (1930), p. 241 ff. On the other features of the rescript, see below.

(137) J. Stroux and L. Wenger, *Die Augustus-Inschrift auf dem Markplatz von Kyrene*, Munchen, 1928. A. Von Premerstein, *Klio*, 1928, 162–169.—J. Anderson, *Journal of Roman Studies*, 1927, pp. 33–48 ; 1929, pp. 220 ff.—Von Premerstein suggests that it was a case of alleged knowledge *de salute principis vel summa rei publicae*, gained from divination and entailing a charge of *laesa maietas*. Paul, *Sent.*, V, 29, 3. Wenger, *op. cit.*, p. 72, explains the case on the basis of *Dig.* 48, 19, 6, where Ulpian recommends what course should be taken by a proconsul when a condemned person, in order to escape punishment, claims to have information concerning the safety of the Emperor (" dicat se habere quod principi referat salutis ipsius causa ").

[138] Ruinart, *Acta Sincera*, p. 217: "Diu sacrilega mente vixisti et plurimos nefariae tibi conspirationis homines aggregasti, et inimicum te diis romanis et sacris legibus constituisti." Quoted by Leclercq, "Droit persécuteur," *Dictionnaire d'archéologie chrétienne et de liturgie*, fascicule XL, col. 1593, note 10.

[139] In order to account for the persecution of Christianity one may not neglect the role played by popular belief encouraged by enemies in ascribing various crimes such as infanticide, treason to the Christians. We may call this the *fortuitous* factor in the process. The theory first enunciated by Le Blant was restated by M. Conrat, *Die Christenverfolgungen in römischen Reich vom Standpunkte der Juristen*, Leipzig, 1897.

[140] Suetonius, *Nero*, Ch. XLIX: Tertullian, *Apologet*, XXV, XXXV, XXXVII.

[141] Aurelius Victor, *De Caesaribus*, C. XVII.

[142] *Cod. Theod.*, 1, IX, *tit*. XVI, *lex* 6, *De malef*.

[143] A. Profumo, *Le fonti ed i tempi dello incendio neroniano*, Rome, 1905, pp. 197–353. The three crimes united under one head were ones published in (*a*) Leges sumptuariae Juliae, (*b*) lex Julia de peculatu et de sacrilegis, (*c*) lex Julia de maiestate imminuta.

[144] Cuq, *Dict. des ant. gr. et rom.*, IV, p. 984.

[145] Mommsen, "Der Religionsfrevel," *Hist. Zeit.*, 1890, p. 409.

[146] Mommsen, *Röm. Str.*, 568, 579. See above.

[147] Mommsen, "Der Religionsfrevel," p. 392, 393. See above.

[148] Tacitus, *Annales*, I, 73. Mommsen, *Röm. Str.*, p. 580, note 1.

[149] Mommsen, *Röm. Str.*, p. 578.

[150] Dio, 47, 18. Mommsen, *Röm. Str.*, p. 568, calls it "the violent measure of a monarchical reaction." Yet the municipalities of Syria and of Asia minor imposed such a duty on citizens. Cf. case of Jews at Antioch. Josephus, *B. Jud.*, 7, 3, 3.

(151) *Lex Ursonensis*, LXVI, in Bruns, *Fontes Juris Romani Antiqui*, 7 ed., Tübingen, 1909, p. 125 : " De auspiciis quaeque ad eas res pertinebunt augurum jurisdictio judicatio esto."

(152) Mommsen, *Juristiche Schriften*, vol. 1, p. 251, regards it as a slip. One should also not forget the rights which the Pontifex Maximus had over the Vestal Virgins. In case of neglect or misbehaviour on their part, he could inflict any sentence up to and including death on them and on those involved with them in the offence. Cf. Girard, *Organisations judiciaires*, p. 37.

(153) Strachan-Davidson, *Problems*, I, p. 26–27.

(154) Cicero, *Pro Caecina*, XXXIV : " Ut religione civitas solvatur." It is usually held that the civil jurisdiction, though absorbing the religious, never bothered in later times to punish the religious offense. There is a fundamental inconsistency in such a state of affairs with the situation in early times.— Tacitus, *Annales*, I, 73, 5 : " Jusiurandum perinde aestimandum quam si Jovem fefelisset ; deorum iniurias dis curae." This refers only to injury in the form of a false oath ; that the gods, however, were not regarded as passive is indicated by the invocation of the fetial, " tum illo die, Juppiter, populum Romanum sic ferito ut ego hunc porcum hic hodie feriam." Livy, I, 24, 8.

(155) For the general view adopted in the following lines, see Maine, *Ancient Law* (Everyman's Library), Chapter X. Subject to correction in detail, Maine's conclusions may still be accepted. For criticism, see Strachan-Davidson, *Problems of Roman Crim. Law*, I, 36, 58, 131 ; II, 16, 42. Cf. the notes of Sir F. Pollock on Maine's *Ancient Law*, London, 1932.

(156) Maine believed that only the *comitia centuriata* had the right to pass sentence (*Anc. Law*, p. 228), thus ignoring the role of the magisterial *imperium*. The latter, represented by the *ius coercitionis*, was, however, extensive throughout the Republic and, though curtailed for a while by the rise of the jurisdiction of *quaestiones perpetuae*, nevertheless came into its own again in the Empire. Mommsen has called this new *coercitio* a " coercitionartige judication," possessing

elements both of the old unlimited power of the magistrate and the newer court procedure. See Callewaert, *Revue d'hist. eccles.*, 1901, t. II, pp. 772–774. That both the procedure *extra ordinem* (before the magistrate), and the procedure before a jury court continued in the early years of the Empire is revealed by the choice given the Greeks in Cyrene (in the fourth edict 11, 65–66), of either form of trial. Stroux and Wenger, *op. cit.*, p. 110. περί των ὑποδίκων κεφαλῆς αὐτὸς διαγεινώσκειν καί ἱστάναι ἤ συνβούλιον κριτῶν παρέχειν ὀφείλει.

Jour. Rom. Stud., t. XIX, p. 222. Most students agree that *quaestio* and *cognito* were alternative, against Von Premerstein, who construes κεφαλῆς in sense of *caput*, so that reference would, according to him, be to (*a*) Capital cases (before *quaestio*), (*b*) Less serious cases involving loss of citizenship or of freedom (before *cognito*).—In support of the common view Stroux quotes Dig. I, 18, 8–9 : " Eum (qui provinciae praeest) aestime debere ipse cognoscere an iudicem dare debeat."

(157) Maine, *Anc. Law*, p. 226.

(158) W. S. Ferguson, " The Lex Calpurnia," *Journal of Roman Studies*, 1921, 86.

(159) Cumont, *Rev. hist.*, 1930, p. 241. Up to recently it was believed that *sepulchri violatio* was a matter of civil redress and that in the second century a jurisconsult applied the *Lex Julia de vi publica* to the offence together with a capital sentence. The inscription found in Palestine and recently brought to the attention of scholars by Rostovtsef and Cumont shows that the death penalty was the rule under Augustus, unless, as Mitteis suggests, it was a conception of Greek law adopted by Rome, *Reichsrecht und Volksrecht*, 1891, p. 100 ff. Cumont finds evidence of the punishment of *violatio sepulchri* in old Roman law. The edict of Julian which is apparently based on old Roman law makes *violatio sepulchri* an offense *manium vindice poena*, which is replaced in *Cod. Just.*, by the words *proxima sacrilegio.*—Of the same mind is M. Morel, " Le Sepulchrum," *Annales de L'Université de Grenoble*, V, 1928, p. 5–180.—The history of the crime of *violatio sepulchri* thus has three stages (*a*) punished by community ; (*b*) a matter

of civil redress, the praetor granting an action of *violatio sepulchri ;* (c) under Augustus the offence was again punished by the State. Are we to ascribe the same development to the religious crime ? The evidence cited elsewhere may well lead us to doubt the existence of a second stage in the *crimen laesae religionis.* But the continuity in the history of one crime offers an instructive analogy to that of the other.

(160) For this class of crimes see the appropriate title in the *Digest,* XLVII, II. Such offences as defiling water sources, performing abortion and seducing minors fall under this head. Strachan-Davidson, *Problems,* II, 162. Rein, *Criminalrecht,* p. 108 (cited by Strachan-Davidson) : " These offences were so called because they were not originally regarded as offences or at least not as criminal misdemeanours." In case any culprit slipped through the toils of the law, still another classification of crime was established, *stellionatus.* Ulpian, *Digest,* XLVII, 20, 3, 1.

(161) Maine, *Anc. Law,* p. 231.

(162) See text above and notes 136, 159.

(163) It should be clear, of course, that though actionable, the offence was not always prosecuted. A good deal depended on the individual magistrate. In the last days of the Republic when civil war was the order of the day it is not inconceivable that magistrates did not take this duty more seriously than other duties.

(164) G. Wissowa, " Law, (Roman) ", Hastings, *Enc. of Rel. and Eth.,* VII, p. 884.

(165) How far the duty of the magistrate entered into the pictures has been differently decided by students. Girard, *Organisations judiciaires,* p. 29, note 1, believes that both the magistrate and the private individual shared the responsibility of shunning or pursuing (as the case might be) the culprit. Against Mommsen, Strachan-Davidson, *op. cit.,* I, pp. 8 ff. believes that the *sacer homo* was one who could be killed with impunity.

[166] The instrumentality of human hands is denied by some scholars. See Brunnenmeister, *Tödtungsverbrechen*, p. 152. The texts, however, disprove this view. Cf. Macrob., *Sat.*, III, 7, 5; Horace, *Odes*, III, 23, 9.

[167] Cicero, *Pro Tullio*, 47: "Legem antiquam de legibus sacratis quae iubent impune occidi eum qui tribunum plebis pulsaverit." Livy, III, 55, 7, "et eius caput Iovi sacrum esset, familia ad aedem cereris, Liberi, Liberaeque venum iret." Cf. Dion. Hal, VI, LXXXIX, 3.—Wissowa, *loc. cit.*, VII, p. 885.

[168] Wissowa, *loc. cit.*, p. 884.

[169] Mommsen uses the supposed breakdown in religion and in politics as a foil to elevate Caesar. Cf. article in *Hist. Zeit.*, XL, p. 390. Cf. Boissier, *La Religion romaine d'Auguste aux Antonins*, I, chapter I.

[170] Ferrero, *Characters and Events of Roman History*, Boston, 1907, chapter I.

[171] Augustine, *De Civ. Dei*, IV, 27.

[172] W. Kroll, *Neue Jahrbucher für Paedagogik*, 1928, pp. 519-31.

[173] See especially A. D. Nock, *Class. Review*, t. 39, 1925, pp. 60-67; V. Marchioro, *Rivista d'Italia*, XXXI, 1928, 412-430. Both writers regard the work of Augustus as a sincere reflection of the Emperor's interests. Augustus was probably a superstitious person, as the literary evidence of his age attests. E. Burriss, *Classical Weekly*, XXI, 49-57, (for a study of Horace). C. Pascal in *Rendiconti del r. Instituto Lombardo di scienze e lettere*, 1924, 713-724. E. Haight, *Classical Journal*, XVII, 365-376.

[174] Dill, *Roman Society from Nero to Marcus Aurelius*, ch. I.

[175] C. J. Laing, *Amer. Jour. of Archaeology*, 1914, 80-84.

[176] Juster, *Les Juifs*, I, 245.

CHAPTER THREE

JUDÆA

THE influence of Judæa as a national centre on Jews in the Diaspora differs with the perspective from which one views it. In a spiritual sphere this influence never loses its vigour throughout the period with which we are dealing. Jews never cease to look to Jerusalem for religious guidance even during the sad aftermaths of the wars of 66–70 and of 132–135. In fact, these disasters to the national ideal only serve to intensify the religious feelings and forms that still bear its imprint. But this new national orientation, as we shall see, has little in common with the influences which inspired it.

I. Judaism originally a national system rather than a religion.

A good deal of misunderstanding has come from regarding Judaism exclusively as a religion[1] It was more than a religion in Judæa. It was, as students have described it, a " way of life." It comprehended not only a fundamental law but a collection of regulations and practices that could only express themselves in a political sphere. For example, the Jewish court was as much a part of Judaism as the first book of the Pentateuch, and a Jewish court could only function adequately when the Jews possessed political independence.[2] When Jews moved to another environment they naturally had to give up part of their religious observance, for it was often impossible to transfer at the same time an elaborate sacrificial system and an extensive criminal jurisdiction to the Greek cities in which they settled in large numbers. The religious institution which was characteristic of this new status of Judaism in the Diaspora was the synagogue which thus became the medium of adaptation to the new non-national order of things.[3] Not that the Jews did not retain part of their national system in the Greek cities of Asia Minor and in Egypt, for several of the Hellenistic monarchs guaranteed them an extensive autonomy in community affairs.[4] Even this, however, was impossible when the Diaspora reached Italy. For though Rome consented to maintain the *status quo* in the East,[5] she, nevertheless, demanded that the Judaism practised by Roman citizens in Italy be shorn of national features. It was in response to this demand that the Jews of Rome, instead of possessing one communal organization, as was the case in most cities in the East, organized separate synagogues on the model of *collegia*.[6] This was due to the fact that Roman citizenship was exclusive and did not tolerate the practice of foreign national rites by members of the state.

II. *Change in character of Judaism resulting from its passage from East to West.*

In this respect the Roman system was much more exacting than that in vogue in the Hellenistic centres where multiple citizenship was very often encouraged.[7] It may be stated that the farther west Judaism moved the less national it had to be and the less national it actually became. The Jewish settlement in Rome thus marks an important transition from the politico-religious order of the East to the more purely religious community with which we are familiar in our day. For our own problem this evolution is of tremendous importance; in effecting the transition Judaism altered its character so fundamentally that the Roman government could with equanimity regard its status as distinct from that of Judaism in the East and license its institutions accordingly. For the Jews of the West, the bond with Judæa and the national system it represented became, by this arrangement, only a spiritual tie.

The role of Judæa in the political sphere proper also affected the Jews of the East and the West unequally. In the case of both classes, the dominant fact that coloured and at the same time assured their later position was the treaty of alliance entered into between Rome and Judæa in 161 B.C. (and renewed thereafter at intervals).[8]

III. *Effects of fœdus on Jews in Rome and in the East.*

So far as it concerned Rome the existence of such a *fœdus* rendered the possession of Judæan nationality by a Roman citizen impossible. This was in accord with the old Roman principle that only a state possessing a *libertas* of its own could cancel the citizenship of a Roman who had recourse to it as a fugitive from Italy. In other words, a state not in treaty relations with Rome was not presumed, according to the letter of the law, to have a juridical existence.[9] The fact that Judæa had such an existence made it impossible for Jews to be Roman citizens, unless they first surrendered their Jewish nationality. The influence of Judæa, therefore, from this point of view would appear to have been negative and unfavourable.

The influence of Judæa in imparting a status to Jews in the Diaspora and within its own borders, though extensive, may be exaggerated. Let us trace the main features of Judæan history from the point of view of their national importance.

Within the first century of Judæa's relations with Rome, a Roman general entered Jerusalem as a conqueror. He and his successor made the erstwhile friend and ally pay the costs of this expedition.[10] This conquest and the tribute it entailed were by no means the last of the measures adopted by the Roman generals and their successors, the Emperors, to assure Rome a favourable balance in the little country. The war of 66–70 also resulted in the imposition of a tribute, the famous *didrachma*.[11] In 132–135, the Roman armies were again reducing rebel strongholds in Judæa.[12] We may well imagine that with every successive defeat Judæa was shorn of certain attributes of sovereignty until there were few or none left to her. Every defeat also involved the division of the country along new lines. The successive eclipse which the national ideal and the national influence thus suffered may be shown in the two systems with which Rome experimented in Judæa, the province system and the king system.

The conquest of 63 B.C. probably did not make Judæa a province or a part of a province.[13] It did, however, change her status from that of a secular to a sacerdotal state.[14] True to the policy of *Divide et*

78

impera, Gabinius, the successor of Pompey, divided the former kingdom into five self-administering units while withdrawing from the high priest, Hyrcanus, the latter's secular privileges.[15] When Judæa did finally become a province in A.D. 6, the transition was by no means abrupt. The area of this province, ruled by prefects and then by procurators,[16] varied from time to time, but at no time did it approximate the limits attained by the Maccabean kingdom at the height of its power. Under the most favoured even of the Herod dynasty, Palestine was given over to the principle of separation and ruled from different centres. The climax to this provincial evolution occurred in 135, when the name of the province was changed to Palestine, a new colony named Ælia Capitolina established on the site of Jerusalem, and Jews forbidden to settle within the enclave of the once sacred city.[17]

If we study the king system to which Rome had recourse occasionally in Judæa we find it equally devoid of significance from a national point of view.[18] It is true that Herod, playing his stakes well, managed to conciliate Cæsar and Augustus in his favour so that he elicited from the former and had confirmed by the latter a set of privileges for the Jews that were to constitute a sort of *Magna Carta* for the members of this religion for a long time to come.[19] But in return for these and other favours, the Herod dynasty undertook to deliver as a *quid pro quo* the submission of the Jews to the Roman yoke. There was little national about the Herodians. They were Idumeans, of an alien race, and thoroughly detested by the people they ruled.[20] Their mission was associated in the popular Jewish mind with two developments, the growth of the authority of Rome and the progress of separatism.

The former is apparent in the withdrawal from the old Jewish high tribunal, the Synhedrion, of capital juris-diction.[21]   The latter is seen in the divisions of Judæa among the different members of the Herod family. Agrippa II, for example, ruled part of Galilee from A.D. 50 to A.D. 100.[22]   It is to be noted that the war of 66–70 did not affect his status, for his troops were found on the side of Titus throughout.

It is difficult to rear on these facts any pretentious theory of national influence.

IV.   Existence of the Jewish " nation " in the restricted sense of term.

When Mommsen and Juster employ the term nation or *gens* to describe the position of Judæa or the Jewish people after 63 B.C., they must obviously employ it in only a limited sense, for the legal *natio* in the sense of a distinct geographical entity possessing a nominal inde-pendence has ceased to exist.   In its stead are several geographical and administrative units ruled at various times by native kings.   After A.D. 6, however, these are puppets comparable to modern colonial princes.   They lack an elementary condition of sovereignty, capital jurisdiction.   They rule but a fraction of Jewry, and even that on the sufferance of the reigning prince at Rome, whose whims they must gratify.   Rome can well dispense with them, as she does at times, but she retains them for the same reason that modern imperialist powers retain native princes ; it is simpler to deal with a prince than with a whole people.   Furthermore, it simplifies the problem of administration and regulation to assume the legal existence of a nation which no longer really exists. The Jewish *natio* exists only through a refinement of the Roman legal system, through the agency of a *fictio*,[23] or fiction.

NOTES

[1] G. F. Moore, *History of Religions*, 2 vols, New York, 1919, Vol. II. Idem, *Judaism in the First Centuries of the Christian Era*, 3 vols, Cambridge, 1927—G. F. Lehmann—Haupt, *Israel, seine Entwickelung im Rahmen der Weltgeschichte*, Tübingen, 1911, pp. 210–242. A. Schlatter, *Geschichte Israels von Alexander dem Grossen bis Hadrian*, 3 Aufl., Stuttgart, 1925.

[2] Hence the hatred of the Pharisees, the party of religious consolidation for Rome. J. Zeiller, *L'Empire romain et L'Eglise* (*Histoire du monde*, ed. E. Cavaignac), Paris, 1928, p. 2.

[3] H. Leclercq, art. "Judaisme," *Dictionnaire d'archéologie chrétienne et de liturgie*, Paris, 1903 ff., fasc. LXXX, col. 142.—Philo, *Quod omnis probus liber*, 12.

[4] Antiochus the Great transported a large number of Jews to Lydia and Phrygia and established them as separate colonies among the natives, cf. F. Josephus, *Antiq. jud.* 1, XII, III, 4.—For the extensive jurisdiction exercised by Jews in Alexandria, see the following chapter.

[5] J. Juster, *Les Juifs dans l'empire romain*, I, 245, n., cf. E. R. Goodenough. *Jewish Law Courts in Egypt*, New Haven, 1929, *passim*, especially pp. 25, 33.

[6] See following chapter.

[7] See following chapter.

[8] I Mac., 822 ss. Though the text cited of the *Senatus consultum* is corrupt; it is probably authentic. Objection to it has been urged on the ground that Rome could not contract a *foedus aequum* in this period. For a discussion of the general problem see E. Taubler, *Imperium Romanum*, I, Leipzig–Berlin, 1914.

—Tenney Frank, *Roman Imperialism*, ch. VIII, however, points out how the old *civitas foederata* was transformed by the political exigencies into the *socius et amicus* (" the self-delusive Roman phrase intended to stretch the fetial law but not to disregard it "). Despite Wilcken's destructive criticism of the treaty, M. Ginsburg, *Rome et La Judée* (Paris, 1928), ch. I, accepts its authenticity on the ground that though Rome might not conclude a *foedus aequum* with any of the large Oriental monarchies, she was permitted to do so with a State like Judæa.—L. Matthaei, " On Classification of Roman Allies," *Classical Quarterly*, I, 1907, p. 182–204, also accepts the authenticity of the treaty of 161 ff. and classes Judæa among the *socii et amici.*—For similar views, cf. Juster, *Les Juifs*, I, p. 130.

(9) Mommsen, *Römisches Staatsrecht*, Leipzig, 1887, III (Abt. I), pp. 47 ff.

(10) Jos., *Ant.*, XIV, 4, 4–5. *Bel. Jud.*, I, 7, 6.—L. Goldschmidt, *Rev. des et Juives*, t. 34, 1897, p. 192, 194.

(11) M. Ginsburg, *Jewish Quarterly Review*, t. XXI, 1931, p. 281 *et seq.* H. Drexler, *Klio*, t. XIX, 1924, p. 277 *et seq.*—See chapter V of present work.

(12) E. Schurer, *Geschichte des jüdischen Volkes im Zeitalter Jesu Christi*, 3–4 aufl., 4 vols, Leipzig, 1901–09, I, pp. 560–704.

(13) As Marquardt held, *Organisation de l'empire romain*, A. Weiss et P. L. Lucas, tr., 2 v., Paris, 1889–92, II, p. 351, cf. Dio Cassius, XXXVIII, 15, 16 ; Eutropius, VI, 14 ; Orosius, VI, 6 ; Livy, Epit., CII ; Strabo, XVI ; Josephus, *Ant.*, XIV, 4, 3.

(14) V. Chapot, *Le Monde romain*, Paris, 1927, p. 248.

(15) H. Graetz, *History of the Jews*, tr. Löwy et alt. Phila., 1893, II, p. 71.

(16) O. Hirschfeld, *Die kaiserlichen Verwaltungsbeamten bis auf Diocletian*, 2 aufl., Berlin, 1905, p. 384.—The officials in question were probably subject to the legates of Syria. Hirschfeld, p. 406.—They seem to have been unimportant individuals.— Schurer, *op. cit.*, I, p. 487, 565 ff.

(17) Schurer, *op. cit.*, I, p. 700.

(18) Nor was it more successful in bringing peace to the country and submission on the part of the people to Rome.—E. Ciaceri, *atti del r. Istituto Veneto di scienze, lettere, e arti,* LXXVI, 2, pp. 687–724.

(19) Juster, *Les Juifs*, I, 213.—Schurer, *op. cit.*, I, p. 543.

(20) W. Otto, *Herodes*, Stuttgart, 1913.

(21) For a discussion of the problem see R. Husband, *The Trial and Death of Jesus*. Princeton.—See Juster, II, p. 157 *et seq.*

(22) Schurer, *op. cit.*, I, p. 549–64.

(23) A " fictio " in old Roman law was a false averment designed to give jurisdiction. Maine, *Ancient Law* (Everyman's Library), p. 15.—Both Augustus and Claudius in confirming the Jewish privileges use the term *ethnos* of the Jews. Unless the word was employed in a purely ethnic sense, a view which does not fit in with the circumstances in this case, as we shall point out, the term implied that the Emperors regarded the Jewish " nation " as existing in some form or other, probably fictional.—Jos., *Ant.*, XVI, 6, 3–7; XIX, 5, 5.—See also the Claudian edict to the Alexandrians in H. I. Bell, *Jews and Christians in Egypt*, London, 1925, pp. 27–28.

CHAPTER FOUR

THE DIASPORA EAST AND WEST

IT was no idle boast of Philo's when in the middle of the first century he declared, in answer to traducers, that the Jews considered whatever country they inhabited as their real fatherland.[1]   It was his way of saying that Palestine no longer exercised a direct political sway over Jews in the Diaspora.[2]   Their assimilation had been facilitated by the existence of numerous communities outside of Palestine which had acquired political rights from the Hellenistic Monarchs.[3]   The Jews had thus embarked on a programme of political integration that could only result in the attenuation of the remaining bonds with the mother country.[4]

Adaptation of the Jews to their environment.

It was natural that Jews should assimilate much in the course of their contact with other peoples.   Examples are not wanting in literary or epigraphic sources of this adaptation.   Jewish life, as depicted in the latter, is shot through with foreign influences.   In Greek centres this influence was Hellenistic ; in Roman centres it was Latin and Greek.[5]   Philo's *De Specialibus Legibus* shows the effects of these diverse currents on Jewish life in a legal sphere. The Roman influence in the treatise is revealed in the treatment of certain acts such as the possession of poison, as capital offences. The influence of Ptolemaic law is shown in the provision condemning to death the murderer of a slave.[6] Nor does the Jewish religion appear to have remained untouched by these new influences. Sects existed which assimilated the Jewish God to Jupiter[7] others to Jupiter Sabazius,[8] still others to Liber and to Saturn.[9] The epitaphs in the Roman Jewish cemeteries often carry the dedication, *Dis Manibus*.[10] There were some Jewish groups, like the Covenanters of Damascus, which had ceased to demand the ceremony of circumcision for admission to Judaism and even admitted partial proselytes to the fold known as *metuentes* and θεοσεβῄς.[11] This extensive social interchange gives some clue to the political interchange between the two orders.

I. *National character of Jewish settlement in the Greek cities.*

Asia Minor was dotted with Jewish congregations of varying types. Most of these, however, originally had a foreign character which set them apart for a long time from the rest of the inhabitants. The term πολιτευμα was applied in this connection to the Jewish communities of Alexandria and Berenike.[12] In other cities Jews formed a *katoikia*, or foreign colony[13] and, in still others constituted an εθνος[14] or λαος[15]. This earlier status as a foreign community, nevertheless, gave way gradually to one that involved less distincness from that of the Greek population. A term which acquired considerable vogue later was that of ουναγωγη, which in its Greek connotation meant the assembly, but in Hebrew usage signified the congregation or community.[16]   Schurer assumes reasonably enough that the latter was the designation when a Jewish community lost its standing of a *katoikia*, and received citizen rights.[17]

Citizenship of Jews in Greek cities only of limited type.

The Jews in many Greek cities enjoyed citizenship. Sardis,[18] Ephesus,[19] Antioch,[20] and Alexandria,[21] to mention but a few, had bestowed this privilege on them, but whether this citizenship was complete is open to question.   For the Jew could, in general, only enjoy full political rights when he participated in the religion which was part of the Greek city's political system, just as it was part of that of every ancient city.   Furthermore there were certain religious observances on his own part that prevented him from discharging the ordinary duties of citizenship. He could not, for example, attend the sessions of court on his sabbath and holidays nor perform military service because this would have involved neglecting certain ceremonies prescribed by his religion.   In order to enjoy citizenship he would have had to be excused from all these requirements.   This smacked too much of privilege, and it is not strange that the Greek city sometimes hesitated to countenance a situation which " combined the right of citizenship with the maintenance of special prerogative for a section of the population."[22]   Reinach concludes that the Jews enjoyed only a special type of citizenship.   In Cyrene, for example, though the Jews claimed *isonomia* (" equality before the law "), they only enjoyed *isotoleia* (" equality in matters of taxation ").[23] Some such distinction may also have prevailed at Alexandria.

Premium put on national organization.

But though granted citizenship, even of a limited type, the Jewish settlement in the Greek city never quite lost its status of a foreign colony. In order to enjoy political rights in Eastern cities Jews often had to be organized into φυλαι or *nationes* of their own.[24] The Greek city refused to take account of them as individuals but only as members of an ethnic group. In other words a premium was apparently put on their national organization. The Jewish community in a city like Antioch had, therefore, even in Roman times, all the characteristics of a corporation. A bequest of the third century refers to it as the *Universitas* of Antioch.[25] The edict of Claudius to the Alexandrians reproaches the Jews of that city for acting as if they constituted a city apart from that of the Greeks, the implication being, that the relations between Jews and non-Jews in Alexandria were governed on some basis other than that implied in a common citizenship, and there is every reason to believe that this status was typical of that of many Jewish communities in the East.[26]

Jurisdiction of Jewish community in the East.

Besides a separate position based on nationality, the Jewish community in the East possessed a separate jurisdiction. The Jewish court figures prominently in the privileges granted by the Hellenistic monarchs and the Romans to the Jews.[27] Nothing reveals the operation of the jurisdiction exercised by these courts so clearly as the system of fines for violation of sepulture. In Smyrna,[28] Hierapolis,[29] Nicomedia,[30] Julia Concordia[31] and Corykos[32] such fines were valid when the testament or codicil of the deceased was deposited in the archives.[33] The Jewish archives had the same legal standing as those of the city in which they were located, and the Jewish court giving effect to them was therefore, endowed with an extensive jurisdiction. The experience of Paul in and outside of Palestine indicates that this jurisdiction included the right in many cases of imposing sentences carrying corporal punishment (as a penalty). It has even been suggested on the basis of a statement in Philo, that the Jewish court of Alexandria could impose a capital sentence and that the Roman authorities overlooked, if they did not exactly countenance, the Jewish community's infliction of the death penalty by application of lynch law.[34] Whatever the case in reference to a capital jurisdiction the fact remains that the Jewish courts exercised powers based on the special national position of the Jewish groups in the Hellenistic cities.

Other groups in Greek city with separate character.

The Jewish communities were not the only ones existing within the fabric of the Hellenistic city that possessed their own status and jurisdiction. The " body of the Greeks " (το των Ελληνων σωμα), mentioned in the Augustan edict of Cyrene, was probably one of the several subdivisions of the city population based on nationality.[35] In reality this grouping by nationality was characteristic of a society in which legal rights had, in general, not been separated from political rights and in which the individual, as a consequence, was in possession of no privileges that could not be identified with those of some national group to which he belonged.[36] Greek law, like that of the early Middle Age was more personal, that is, it applied to persons rather than to territories ; but, unlike other systems based on the personality of law it dealt with the individual only through the medium of a group, that is, it treated him as a corporation sole having a status that was not the product of free choice but of birth. It was left to Rome to apply a different conception in her dealings with individuals.[37]

Jewish settlement in Rome.

The Jewish settlement in Rome probably dates from the second century B.C. We have no definite evidence on this point with the exception of a passage in II *Maccabees*, which describes the plight of Jewish slaves who found their way into the Roman market.[38] Their fate must have been similar to that of those slaves who were brought by Pompey in 63 B.C. from Palestine. Philo tells us that the latter occasioned their masters so much trouble because of their religious scruples that they were compelled to release them.[39] Manumission, in its turn, brought the rights of citizenship and so, within a short time, we find a considerable Jewish community in the city of Rome, plying its trade and making its influence felt politically.[40] That the

Jewish community in Rome, however, dates considerably before 63 B.C. is indicated by the fact that in 53 B.C. they were so influential in the Roman assembly that Cicero, ever the champion of Romanism, was inveighing vehemently but apprehensively against them.[41]. In the years that followed, the ranks of Jewish Roman citizens were swelled by new admissions. Besides manumission, direct conferment on cities and individuals,[42] and a modest campaign of proselytism,[43] operated to increase the number of Jews who had a part in political life.

Effect on the legal position of Judaism.

How did this extension of the franchise and the consequent increase in the political usefulness of the Jews affect the status of the Jewish religion? Could a national privilege any longer account for its position constitutionally? In the Hellenistic centres it was possible for Jews to organize separate communities with their own organization and jurisdiction because Hellenistic law failed to regard the exercise of one citizenship and nationality as exclusive, as incompatible with the possession of another. A Jew could, figuratively speaking, be at one and the same time a member of the Jewish nation in Palestine, of the Jewish *politeuma* in Alexandria, and perhaps a citizen of the latter city in addition. Such a situation, however, would have been anomalous at Rome where the exclusiveness of the franchise was a premise of all public law. A national privilege could obviously not account for the Jews' position in Rome. What did account for it, therefore? The answer to this question is given by Tertullian

when he refers to Judaism as a " *religio certe licita.*"[44]
A *religio licita* was a religion which citizens were authorized to practice, and Judaism, by becoming one, had
had to lose much of its older national character. This
is revealed by a study of the Jewish communal institutions in Rome.

II. *Jewish community in Rome compared with that of Alexandria or Antioch.*

In that city the Jews were organized in private
societies comparable to those of other religious and
professional groups. Unlike the situation in Alexandria, where the Jews formed one community, the Jewish
synagogues of Rome were separate organizations unconnected with each other except by social bonds.[45]
Each was an institution in its own right possessing
without doubt all the attributes of a corporation or a
collegium.[46] The synagogue is, in fact, described as
such an association in one of the documents.[47] Each
synagogue had its own founder or sponsor, in some
cases an official ; the names of the *Augustenses* and the
Agrippenses possibly testify to the official nature of their
sponsorship.[48] Several of the synagogues were
located in special quarters and ministered to geographical
needs, as the names of the *Campenses* and the *Siburenses*
attest.[49] Instead of a single burial ground the Jews
of Rome possessed a number of cemeteries, located,
from motives of convenience, without doubt, near
their respective places of worship.[50] Curiously enough,
the early Christian catacombs show the same type of
dispersion.[51] The distribution of the population is
another feature that distinguishes the Roman Jewish

community from that of Antioch or Alexandria. Jews occupied quarters in Rome as distant as the Trastevere and the Suburra, the Porta Capena and the Campus Martius.[52] All these arrangements show the effects of the status which Roman law had enhanced in the ancient world, that of territoriality.[53] Every person living in a Roman community was subject directly to Roman law; there was no intermediate political status necessary to validate his legal standing. If Rome did take account of combinations, such as *collegia*, they were less political than legal groupings. As a result of this direct contact between the state and the individual the Jewish community in Rome exercised no such jurisdiction as that in vogue in many Eastern cities. The practical effect of this is obvious. A Roman citizen, like St. Paul, could always appeal from any sentence pronounced by a Jewish court to the regular civil tribunal, and thus render futile the pains of the religious tribunal.

Romans retain original system in Eastern cities

It is worth noting that the Hellenistic arrangement at Alexandria and other cities was maintained intact by Rome which thus gave official assent to a dyarchy in the legal as well as the political realm.[54] Roman law, it is to be noted, did not always *supersede* the law of the countries it subjected to its sway; more often it *supplemented* it and absorbed from it new elements which passed by stages from the *ius gentium* into the civil law. We have noticed such a development in the case of *origo*, a notion which Augustus officially consecrated when he ordered Roman citizens in Cyrene to assume the duties of local citizenship.[55]   Applied to the Jews, this dyarchic system meant that Rome dealt with the *national* people in the East and with the individual citizen in the West.

III.   *Effect of this political evolution on the social and religious life of the Jews.*

As a pendant to this sketch of Jewish political development in the Diaspora, some description may not be amiss of the effect on social life of this evolution from a national to a religious system.

Anti-semitism in the East and the West.

As a result of their greater national homogeneity the Jews of the East were objects of more systematic recrimination than their brethren of the West. With their heavy concentration of population in the Hellenistic cities it was only natural for them to act in a way calculated to provoke the neighbouring population. Claudius, in his edict, reproaches them for the indifference they displayed toward their Greek fellow citizens. The intense resentment which was thus engendered in the Greek inhabitants took several forms.   In the first place it led to an organized and systematic campaign of anti-semitism.   This was encouraged by the fact that the Jews were habitually favourable to the Roman regime and their neighbours were not.[56]   The favour accorded by one Emperor to a Jewish prince led to demonstrations that had repercussions in Palestine and in Rome[57]   The main influence, however, that caused anti-semitism to take such firm root in the East was that the national or quasi-national position of Judaism in these parts produced a counter-national-consciousness in the general population that has in every age been an important element in Judophobia. Apion, the classic exponent of Alexandrian Jew-baiting, whose arguments are familiar to us through the good offices of his opponent, Josephus, asks with acrimony, " Why, if the Jews are citizens, do they not worship the same gods as we ?"[58] These words reflect the attitude of a society which tolerated national differences but was not resigned to the system. From incitement to action is never a long step, and under Caligula, Claudius, Nero, Trajan and Hadrian, sanguinary riots convulsed the two populations in the larger cities of Asia Minor and Egypt. The fear of Jewish revolts was always a weighty factor in the East. The edict of Claudius, which speaks ambiguously of the community's " fomenting a pest common to mankind,"[59] Petronius' reasons for delaying the introduction of a statue of the Emperor in the Temple,[60] the words of Philo to Caligula, which hint of an " insurmountable war " in the event of the adoption of certain measures,[61] all attest the great power with which Rome and the Greek cities had to deal in the East. This power was international in its effects, but its inspiration and incentive were national.

If we contrast this situation with that in Italy and other places where Jews enjoyed Roman citizenship in large numbers, we are struck by the fact that opposition to the Jews did not take the form of systematic Jew-baiting. This was due to the fact that the Jewish position in Latin centres was non-national. It is significant that Cicero, unlike Apion, does not, in his oration for Flaccus, question the citizen rights of the

Jews or their right to be in the assembly. At their worst the Latin writers display toward the Jews a good-natured contempt often mixed with curiosity.[62] At their best some writers show a positive inclination if not preference for Jewish rites. Horace and Ovid give us examples of the latter attitude.[63] Judaism appears to have enjoyed a much wider vogue among eclectics in Rome than in Alexandria, or in Antioch, because in its non-national form it was much less un-palatable to the gentile population. As a result the bloody riots of the Eastern cities between Jews and non-Jews were not re-enacted in Rome. The counter-nationalism which the geographically compact, national-istic, jurisdictional group of Alexandria provoked found less kindling wood in Rome where no condition was favourable to its growth. Occasionally a Jewish group, organized in a synagogue or a trade association, became turbulent; in that case the government meted out the same treatment as it did to disorderly associations in general: it withdrew the *coire licet*, the right of reunion.[64] But of anti-semitism in the sense of a movement based on race or nationality Rome was ignorant.

The differences between the Jewish communities of East and West, and of Palestine and the East were reflected in other small ways. In Palestine the Jews were excused from taxes on the Sabbatical years, thus enabling them to observe the Biblical interdict against sowing in the seventh year.[65] We know of no such arrangement outside of Palestine. In addition to this change, the Jews outside of Palestine seem to have relaxed their traditional iconophobia. Whereas in Palestine the use of Imperial money bearing the image of the Emperor, and all statues of the gods were for-bidden, there was no objection to their use outside of

Palestine.[66]   Buckles and crown-bearing devices were tolerated in the synagogues outside of Palestine, though tabooed in the Holy Land.[67]   All these facts point to a profound and far-reaching evolution in the social and religious life of the Jewish people.

Conclusion.

The point which deserves especial emphasis in conclusion is that the Jewish position both in the Hellenistic world with its notion of nationality divorced from territoriality, which the Romans retained indigenously, and in the Roman world with its rigorous doctrine of national exclusiveness, assumed a form constitutionally in conformance with its environment.

NOTES

[1] Philo Judaeus, *In Flaccum*, 7.

[2] See preceding chapter and Moore, *Judaism in the First Centuries*, II, p. 113 : " Fidelity to their religion and the authority of the interpreters of the law had completely displaced political loyalty and the sense of civic duty." Cf. the statement of Paul, *Rom.*, 13, 1 : " Let every man be in subjection to the authorities that are set over him ; for no authority exists unless by God's will, so that one who arrays himself against the authority puts himself in opposition to the ordinance of God, and those who oppose this will bring on themselves (God's) judgment." Compare the words of Rabbi Jose ben Kisma to Hanina ben Teradion, in *Aboda Zora*, 18a : " You know, my brother, that this people (the Romans) has been given the kingdom by heaven." In the same vein Rabbi Simeon ben Lakish construed the verses from Genesis, " Behold, it was good " ; and, " I created Adam (Edom,

Rome) over it." These statements are from Hadrian's time. As an example of Jewish conformance, Moore cites the sacrifices performed for the Emperor in the Temple. *Op. cit.*, II, p. 115. The supposed correspondence between the king of Lacedaemon and the Jewish High Priests (Macc. 12, 20-23 ; Jos. *Ant.*, XII, XIII), might have been the work of Hellenizing Jews anxious to adapt themselves to their environment. S. Jebelief in *Comptes rend. de l'Acad. des sciences rus.*, 1928, p. 65-70, abstracted by Marrouzeau, *Année philologique*, 1929.

(3) Josephus, *Ant.*, XII, 31, says that Seleucus I (Nikator), granted the right of citizenship to Jews in all cities founded by him.

(4) In age and in the proportion of population settled outside of Palestine, the Diaspora compared favourably with the mother country. In the history of the Diaspora and its origins in the pre-exilic period, see A. Causse in *Revue d'histoire et de philosophie religieuse*, 1927, p. 97-128. On population, see Juster, I, p. 210. For general surveys of Diaspora, see Juster, I, p. 180-209 ; Schurer, art. " Diaspora," in Hastings' *Dictionary of the Bible*, supplementary volume, p. 100 *et seq.* ; Leclercq, art. " Judaisme," *Dict. d'arch. chrét. et de litur.*, T. VIII, cols. 1-254 ; T. Reinach, art. " Judaei," t. III., pt. 1, p. 623, *Dict. des ant. gr. et rom.* ; art. " Diaspora," *Jewish Encyclopedia*, New York, 1903, *et seq.*

(5) J. Reill, *Rev. des et. juives*, t. LXXII, p. 24-28. For the resemblance in characters between a Jewish inscription of Sardinia and the *grafitti* found at Pompeii, see J. Chabot, in *Museon : Revue d'etudes orientales*, 1921, 107-110. An analysis of the language of the Jewish inscriptions at Rome shows that the speech of the Jews did not differ from that of the general population. The Greek v was pronounced like Y ; $\alpha\iota$ was pronounced like ϵ. H. J. Leon, *Transactions and Proceedings of the American Philological Association*, 1927, p. 210-233. The same writer, however, draws the conclusion that the Jews formed a closed population in Rome, H. J. Leon, *Jewish Quarterly Review*, vol. XX, p. 301-312. Our literary and epigraphic evidence, nevertheless, points to the dispersion of Jews and Jewish beliefs among the population.

(6) See E. R. Goodenough, *Jurisprudence of the Jewish Courts in Egypt* for discussion.

[7] S. Augustine, *De Consensu Evangelist.*, I, 27; Origen, *Contra Celsum*, I, XXIV.

[8] See above and Cumont, art. " Sabazius," *Dict. des ant. gr. et rom.*, IV, p. 929–930.

[9] Plutarch, *Sympos*; 4, 5; Tacitus, *Histor.*, V, 5; Tibullus, *Eleg.*, I, XIII, 18; Dio Cassius, *Hist.* XXXVII, XVI, 2. Cf. Leclercq, *Dict. d'arch. chrét*, VIII, col. 102.

[10] N. Muller and N. A. Bees, *Die Inschriften der Judischen Katacombe am Monteverde zu Rom*, Leipzig, 1919, no. 43. Reinach, in *Rev. des et juives*, LXXI, p. 114 *et seq.*, believes it is a pagan epitaph, but if so, how did it and others of its type find their way into a Jewish catacomb?

[11] For covenanters see note in preceding chapter. For word θεοσεβης, see epitaph in Vogelstein and Rieger, *Geschichte der Juden in Rom*, Leipzig, 1895, vol. I, no. 41. The Empress Poppaea Sabina is described by Josephus as θεοσεβης, Josephus, *Ant.* XX, 8, 11; *Vita*, 3. For the use of the term *metuens*, see Vogelstein and Rieger, I., nos. 141, 170, 173, 197; and *Corp. Inscr. Lat.*, t. V, no. 88; t. VIII, no. 4321. Whether these terms signified an intermediate stage in the practice of Judaism comparable to that of the *catachumen* in Christianity, as Leclercq (t. VIII, col. 110, *Dict. d'arch. chrét.*) maintains or whether they represented an abberration from Judaism it is difficult to say. Rabbinic writings make no use of these terms or ones implying a similar status. For a study of evolution of religious ideas in Rabbinic literature and how change was often accomplished by means of legal fictions, see S. Zuckrow, *Adjustment of Law to Life in Rabbinic Literature*, Boston, 1932. Cf. also article " Judaism," by H. Loewe, *Hastings' Enc. of Rel. and Eth.*, vol. VII, p. 592.

[12] *Aristeae Epist.*, ed. Wendland, no. 310; *Corp. Inscr. Gr.*, 5, 5361. A *politeuma* is mentioned in an inscription of Cos that may have been Jewish; see Perdrizet, *Revue archéologique*, 1899, t. XXXV, p. 44.

[13] The term was used in Hierapolis, Leontopolis. Josephus, *Ant.*, XIII, 3, 1. Schurer, in *Hastings' Dict. of the Bible*, sup. volume, p. 101, and G. Cardinaldi, *Note di terminologia epigrafica* in *Rendiconti dell' Accademia dei Lincei*, 1908, p. 196, both sustain the thesis that the word describes a foreign

98

colony. The fact that Romans were often organized as such groups in Greek cities does not disprove such a view, as Leclercq (art. " Judaisme," *Dict. d'arch. chért*, t. VIII, col. 132) seems to believe.

(14) As at Smyrna, *Rev. des et juives*, 1883, t. VII, p. 161.

(15) As at Mantinea. *Rev. des et. juives*, 1897, t. XXXIV, p. 148. Probably also at Hierapolis, at Nysa, at Smyrna and at Elche. Schurer, *loc. cit.*, p. 101.

(16) For the different *senses* of the word see Latyschev, *Inscr. antiq. Ponti Euxini*, II, nos. 52, 53, which oppose synagogue to *proseuque*, community to edifice. In the sense of community also see its use in Josephus, *Antiq, jud.*, XIX, VI, 3 ; *Bel. Jud*, II, XIV, 4 ; VII, III, 3. See Leclercq, *loc. cit.*, col. 142.

(17) Schurer, *loc. cit.*, p. 101, who cites proofs of his view in inscriptions from Phocaea, Akmonia, and Pantikapaeum.

(18) Josephus, *Ant.*, XIV, 10, 24.

(19) Josephus, *Contra Apionem*, II, 4.

(20) Josephus, *Ant.*, XII, 3, 1, according to whom the privileges of the Jews were inscribed on brass tablets. Cf. *Bel jud.*, VII, 5, 2.

(21) The statement of Josephus (*Contra Ap.*, II, 4 ; *Bel. jud.*, II, 28, 7 ; *Ant.*, XIX, 5, 2), that Alexander put them on a footing of equality with the Greeks does not mean " on a similar footing," as the Claudian Edicts show. See among other treatments, S. Reinach, *Revue d'histoire de religion*, t. 90, 1924, p. 108–122.

(22) T. Reinach, art. " Diaspora," *Jewish Encyclopedia*, p. 567.— Art. " Judaei," *Dict. des ant. gr. et rom.*, t. III, pt. I, p. 624.

(23) *Ibid.*—Jos., *Ant.*, XVI, 5, 1.

(24) Ramsay, *Expositor*, January, 1902, and February, 1902, p. 97.

(25) *Code Justinian*, I, IX, 1. See below.

(26) See the letter in Bell, *Jews and Christians at Alexandria,* and its interpretation by Jouguet in *Journal des savants*, pp. 18–19 : " Et d'autre part, je commande formellement aux Juifs de ne point chercher a augmenter leurs anciens privilèges . . . comme si vous habitiez deux villes differentes." Here Claudius forbids the Jews to send *political* embassies. The

Jewish community at Alexandria, though separate in certain respects from the Greek community, was obviously limited in its political privileges.

(27) Cf. for example, Jos., *Ant.*, XIV, 10, 2.

(28) *Rev. des et juives*, 1883, VII, 161, 1666.

(29) W. Judeich, *Jahrbuch des kaiserlich deutschen archaeologischen Instituts, Erganzungsheft*, 1898, no. 69.

(30) *Echos d'Orient*, 1905, VIII, p. 271.

(31) *Corp. Inscr. Lat.*, V, 8764.

(32) *Inscr. Graecae ad res romanas pertinentes*, III, 858.

(33) Keil, *Hermes*, 1908, XLIII, p. 572, 575.

(34) Philo, *De Spec. Leg.*, 3, 5.—The view is taken by Goodenough, *Jewish Law Courts at Alexandria*. See below.

(35) Anderson, *Journal of Roman Studies*, 1929, p. 221.

(36) W. S. Ferguson, art., " Greek Law," *Encyclopedia Britannica*, 14th ed., New York, 1929, vol. X, p. 829.

(37) Of course, there were precedents for Rome's action in the Greek world. Ferguson, *loc. cit.* : " Historically, there was a connection between political and legal equality and in Athens both were realized on a basis of self-government in 507 B.C. after the expulsion of the Peisistratids. . . . In Boeotia also those owning property became councillors, who alone could transact public business ; but they had no greater rights in private law than freeborn adults."

(38) Cf. also the account of the Jews' expulsion in 139 B.C. Valerius Maximus, I, 3, 2.

(39) Philo, *Leg. ad Caium*, 23.—Cf. Jos., *Ant.*, XVIII, 3, 5 ; Tacitus *Annales*, II, 85.

(40) P. Girard, *Manuel de droit romain*, Paris, 1906, p. 104.—It was not until the time of Augustus (Leges Aelia Sentia ; Furia-Camima), that the political privilege brought by manumission was reduced to that of Latin citizenship.

(41) Cicero, *Pro Flacco*, 28, 66.

(42) As by the successful prosecution of a magistrate for extortion. See *Lex Acilia*, in Bruns, *Fontes*.

(43) It would appear from the scant epigraphic evidence that Jewish proselytism was not so widespread as the literary evidence might lead one to believe. For a judgment on the question see G. La Piana, *Harvard Theological Review*, October, 1927.

(44) Tertullian, *Apologet.*, 21.

(45) T. Reinach, art., " Judaei," *Dict. des ant. gr. et rom.*, tome III, pt. I, p. 625.

(46) For the juridical personality of Jewish communities in general see Juster, I, 424–438.

(47) As θιάσος in Jos., *Ant.*, XIV, X, 8.

(48) See for example Muller and Bees, *op. cit.*, nos. 2, 174 ; Vogelstein and Rieger, *op. cit.*, nos. 176, 120. There is also a *synagoga Bolumni* mentioned (Vogelstein and Rieger, no. 152), which took its name from its sponsor. Were these synagogues founded by the *liberti* of Augustus, Agrippa, and Volumnius ? Cf. E. Bormann in *Wiener Studien*, 1912, vol. XXXIV, pp. 358–269. For the names and number of the synagogues in Rome see especially La Piana, *Harv. Theol. Review*, October, 1927, p. 352, and Leclercq, *Dict. d'arch. chrét.*, VIII, cols. 132–133.

(49) Vogelstein and Rieger, nos. 46, 11 ; 68, 72.—For the Siburenses see *Revue archéologique*, 1921, p. 471, n. 74.—The Jewish catacombs on the *via nomentana* give us frequent mention of this synagogue. See B. Manna, *Bolletino della commissione archaeol. Commun. in Roma*, 1922, 205–223 ; and Paribeni, *Notizie degli Scavi di Ant.*, 1923, pp. 142–155.

(50) For list see Leclercq, *Dict. d'arch. chrét.*, VIII, cols. 184–185.— Whether each synagogue had its own cemetery remains open to question. See also H. Leon, *Hebrew Union College Annual*, V, 1928, 299–314.

(51) Leclercq, *loc. cit.*, col. 184.

(52) Besides the information to be gleaned from names of synagogues and places of burial, see Philo, *Leg. ad Caium*, 23 ; Martial, I, 41 ; XII, 57 ; Juvenal, III, 10–20 ; *Corp. Inscr. Graec.*, IV, nos. 9905, 9906.

(53) H. F. Jolowicz, art., " Roman Law," *Enc. Brit.*, vol. XIX, p. 447.

[54] Josephus, *Ant.*, XII, 3, 1, says that the Hellenistic privileges were confirmed by the Roman authorities as late as the reign of Titus.

[55] See above, second chapter.

[56] U. Wilcken, *Zum Alexandrinischen Antisemitismus*, 1909, p. 45.

[57] When Caligula restored the monarchy in favour of Herod Agrippa. Schurer, *Geschichte des judischen Volkes im Zeitalter Jesu Christi*, I, p. 549-564.

[58] Josephus, *Contra Ap.*, 2, 6: " Quomodo, si sunt cives eosdem deos quos Alexandrini non colunt." Compare these words with those of two Roman writers. " Judaea gens contumeliis numinum insignis " (Pliny, *N. H.*, 13, 4, 46); and " nec quicquam prius imbruuntur quam contemnere deos " (Tacitus, *Hist.*, 5, 5). Apion's concern is with the failure of the Jews to worship the official gods (proof that Judaism was regarded as alien); the concern of Tacitus and Pliny is with the hatred of the Jews for the official gods, not concern about the religion which the Jews themselves were practising, which was presumably permissible.

[59] Bell, *Jews and Christians at Alexandria*, pp. 27-28, cf. also Jos., *Ant.*, XIX, V, 2.

[60] Jos., *Ant.*, XIX, VI, 3.

[61] Philo, *Leg. ad Caium*, 31.

[62] For the views of Horace, Tibullus, Ovid, Perseus, Petronius, Martial Juvenal, see the appropriate pages in T. Reinach, *Textes d'auteurs grecs et romains relatifs au judaisme*, Paris, 1890, *passim*.

[63] According to Lejay, *Revue d'histoire et de littérature religieuses*, 1903, VIII, pp. 305-335, the observance of the Jewish Sabbath was the most characteristic feature of the widespread vogue of Judaism. See also Herbert Strong, *Hibbert Journal*, January, 1915, pp. 300-313.

[64] See chapter six.

[65] Jos., *Ant.*, XIV, X, 56.—Schurer, *op. cit.*, I, p. 37.

[66] Jos., *Ant.*, XVIII, V, 3; XVIII, III; *Bel jud.*, II, IX, 2-3.

[67] Jos., *Ant.*, XIX, V, 2, 3.

CHAPTER FIVE

JUDAISM AS *RELIGIO LICITA*

THERE are two alternatives to assuming the *natio* as the basis of the Jewish *privilegia* in the Roman Empire. First, that the basis of these *privilegia* was a *religio licita* and that this accounted for the religious position of all the Jews in the Empire. Secondly, that both the *natio* and the *religio licita* were each in some measure responsible for some special phase of Jewish religious privilege. In this arrangement the *religio licita* would apply to the *status civitatis* and the *natio* would apply to the *peregrini*. That there was a distinction between the treatment meted out to Jews in the western part of the Empire, where most of them enjoyed Roman citizenship, and the treatment of those in the East, who were still *peregrini*,[1] was clearly recognized by Mommsen who, however, contented himself with remarking that while their status in the East was clearly delineated, their religious position in the West was very precarious and probably devoid of a legal basis.[2]

I. Distinction between religio licita and natio.

We ventured to suggest in an earlier part of the paper that the Eastern arrangement in regard to the

Jews was essentially the arrangement that had existed in Hellenistic times, and that the Romans had in turn sanctioned this situation because it was part of their policy in the East not to increase unduly the magnitude of their task of government. We pointed out at the same time that this arrangement could hardly apply to Jews in Italy and other parts of the Empire where they enjoyed citizenship in large numbers.

II. Theories of Mommsen and of Juster.

It is a distinction which Mommsen and his immediate followers have failed to recognize adequately. For the period before the year A.D. 70, for example, Mommsen makes the *natio* the sole recipient of the religious *privilegia*, thus ignoring completely the legal position of the Jewish *cives Romani*. The latter in his view were practising, prior to 70, a religion to which as Roman citizens they had no right, a fact of which the government occasionally took cognizance by expelling them from the city of Rome or cancelling their " right of assembly."[4]

The year 70 in Mommsen's eyes introduced a change in the position of both classes of Jews (*cives Romani* and *peregrini*). According to him *all* the Jews of the Empire became *dediticii*, and lost the right to their national religion.[5] In order, therefore, to account for the religious toleration which the Jews enjoyed after 70 Mommsen postulated a *religio licita* whose concrete basis in law was the Synagogue in the role of a *collegium licitum*. The *civitas Romana* according to him did not save Jews who possessed it from the *status dediticiæ* after 70.[6] The *religio licita*, Mommsen avers, rendered the religious position of the Jewish non-citizen and citizen equal (in so far as after 70 such a distinction exists), and gave the Roman citizen for the first time a religion which was recognized by the state.

Politically, this change from a national to a licensed religion coincided according to Mommsen with the transformation of the Jewish πολιτευμα (quasi independent colony of Jews in a Greek city), into συναγωγη (religious congregation). The Jewish communities in the East, in other words, lost their political character and became *collegia licita*, members of the *religio licita*, and as such enjoying a position that did not depend on the *natio*.[7]

Change of view on Mommsen's part.

Whether the *religio licita* which emerged from the circumstances raised by the year 70 was a licensed religion in the true sense of the term[8] Mommsen is not altogether clear. In his earlier treatment the latter had maintained that the *religio licita* (of the period following 70) was open to proselytes provided they obtained the necessary licence and paid the proper tax.[9] The licence, according to him, was necessary only for those who desired to become members of the synagogues ; it was not obligatory on those who practised their Judaism in private. The tax which the Jewish religionists had to pay for permission to practice their rites was the well-known *didrachma* which Vespasian had imposed on the Jews (apparently all Jews) after the fall of Jerusalem.[10] The proceeds of this tax were diverted to the treasury of Jupiter Capitolinus and were, therefore, apparently in the nature of a tribute to the state cult. The tax was imposed on the confession and as the confession was thus licensed it was open even to proselytes. It was in this way that Mommsen interpreted the following passage from Suetonious : " Præter ceteros Judaicus fiscus acerbissime actus est ; ad quem deferebantur qui vel *improfessi* Judaicam viverent vitam, vel, dissimulata origine, imposita *genti* tributa non perpendissent. Interfuisse me adulescentulum memini, cum a procuratore frequentissimoque consilio inspiceretur nonagenarius senex, an circumsectus esset."[11] Hardy, following Mommsen, assumes that Domitian was (in the sense of the passage) violating precedent when he subjected to the *Fiscus Judaicus* not only those who belonged to the Jewish confession but even those who were not officially enrolled in the synagogue, though they practised their religion in private.[12]

Mommsen subsequently, however, modified his stand on the confessional position of Judaism.[13] In the face of a mass of evidence which clearly showed the hostility of the Roman government toward proselytism, and the frequent charges of atheism levelled against Romans accused of practising Jewish religious rites,[14] Mommsen altered his view of the strictly confessional legal basis of Judaism, by conceding that membership in the Jewish religion might have been subject to ethnic conditions. Judaism, in other words, was a sort of hereditary confession closed to outsiders.

In all this, it is evident that Mommsen's mainspring is his theory that after the year 70 the Jewish nation as such was juridically extinct. An inscription of the time of Hadrian found at Smyrna, which speaks of οι ποτε Ιουδαιοι (" those who were once Jews "), is his main documentary support for this contention. That this inscription can be interpreted in a variety of ways other than the one to which Mommsen puts it is indicated by Juster.[15]   Juster affirms that if the *status dediticiæ* was imposed on the Jews after the year 70, it affected only a part of them and even these not for a long time.   He rejects emphatically the view that Roman citizens and citizens of Greek cities were made *edidticii*.   He proves beyond a reasonable doubt that the Jewish " nation " existed subsequent to the year 70, and if we understand the word nation in the limited sense we have given it, we may agree with him.[16]

Connotation of term " Judæi."

But in his rejection of Mommsen's thesis Juster goes to the other extreme.   He makes the position of the Jews after as before the year 70 (to Juster this year is devoid of significance) depend entirely on the *nation*. Like Mommsen he fails or refuses to discern any distinctions in the *privilegia* based on considerations of *civitas* and *peregrinitas*.   In this vein he criticizes Mommsen's use of the term *Judæi* after the year 70.[17] Before this year, according to Mommsen, the term had a national or purely ethnic connotation, but after the year 70 it took on a confessional meaning.   Juster, arguing from the obvious connection of the word with Judæa asserts that it could only have had a national signification.   There is no other term, as a matter of fact, commonly employed to designate members of the Jewish religion all through Roman history.   Its use cannot be regarded from a critical point of view as an argument for either side.   The same is true of the concomitant fact which Juster cites, namely that the inscriptions never mention the community or synagogue to which the deceased belonged, but merely the fact that the latter is a " Jew, i.e. member of the Jewish nation."[18]   Here Juster is rebutting Mommsen's view that the Jews after 70 belonged to their respective *collegia* (synagogues) and not the *natio*.

Allusion to community in Jewish tomb inscriptions.

Juster, besides not being altogether correct in his statement, fails to distinguish between the legal, Roman aspect of the Jews' position which made them members of their particular *collegia*, and the Jews' own view, which left them as always, members of the chosen nation, brethren in all lands.   Jewish tomb inscriptions would depict only the latter phase of Jewish life.   Besides being inapplicable, Juster's observation is inaccurate, at least as concerns the Jewish tomb inscriptions found in Rome.   In these the race or nationality of the deceased is mentioned only infrequently, but connection with the synagogue of which the defunct happened to be a member is often recalled, especially in the case of an official of the synagogue.[19]   It is important to note that though references to separate synagogues abound, there is never any allusion to a Jewish community in Rome.   In this regard the situation at Rome differed from that of most Eastern cities, where a single community was ordinarily the rule.   This difference, as we have indicated, was a reflection of the varying influences that operated in both sections.

III.   *The Acta of Josephus.*

A further basis for such a distinction, it appears to this writer, is provided by the various *Acta* in Josephus'

Antiquities. Where Josephus obtained them, whether from the archives at Rome or from some writer like Nicolaus of Damascus, is a question that scholars pronounce, with some reason, insoluble.[20] Though they are cited from motives frankly apologetic and are designed to present the Jew in as enviable a light as possible, and though an occasional corruption or error in copying may be detected by the scholar, the essential authenticity of these *Acta* has never been successfully questioned. When we reflect that these *Acta* represent the whole extent of our knowledge of the laws governing the Jews in the Empire, it is evident that they repay careful study.[21] No other similar collection of laws on the Jews is extant: the sections dealing with the Jews in the Jurisconsults have not come down to us.

In the *Acta* which follow, special privileges are granted to various groups of the Jewish population and to the grant of each class a special reason or explanation is given.

Distinction between the religion and the nation in the privileges.

Thus, privileges which are granted to Jews who are Roman citizens are given on the basis of their cult. Privileges which are granted to members of the Jewish nation are given because " they are our friends and allies." At the same time there is also a rough distinction made between the duties from which *cives Romani* and *Jewish allies* are respectively exempted. In the case of the Roman citizen, it is usually military service, a typical citizen requirement, from which exemption is granted. In the case of the allied Jewish nationals the exemption is from attendance at the law courts on the Sabbath and holidays. Is it fanciful to argue that the Jewish cult (or superstition) for legal purposes, enjoyed a position independent of the Jewish nation? The decrees dealing with Jewish Roman citizens are always careful to avoid mentioning the Jewish nation as responsible for the *privilegia*, thus always making the basis of the grant the " superstition " or " cult ".

The following decree was issued in 49 B.C. by the consul L. Lentulus Crus.[22] In this year the civil war between Pompey and Cæsar had broken out. Lentulus had been entrusted by the Senate with the task of raising two legions in Asia. He it was who issued the decree and addressed it to the Ephesians through his legate, Ampius Balbus.

" Lucius the consul's decree : I have at my tribunal set these Jews who are *citizens of Rome*[23] and follow the *Jewish religious* rites[24] and yet live at Ephesus from going into the army *on account of their religion*."[25][26]

The decree that follows is also from the year 49. It explains itself : " Decree of the Delians : Marcus Piso the legate gave orders that if there be here any *Jews who are Roman citizens*[27] *no one* is to give them any disturbance about going into the army because Cornelius Lentulus the consul freed the Jews from going into the army *on account of their religion*."[28][29] It is possible that the phrase *on account of their religion* has a definite legal connotation. The following decree which is concerned more intimately with the religious position of the Jews shows the same legal form. Its date also is 49 B.C.

" Lucius Antonius, vice-quæstor and vice-prætor to the magistrates, senate and people of the Sardians.

Those Jews that are our *fellow citizens (of Rome)*[30] came to me and *demonstrated* that they had *an assembly of their own*,[31] according to the laws of their forefathers and this from the beginning, as also a place of their own wherein they determined their suits and controversies with one another. Upon their petition therefore to me that these might be lawful for them I give order that these their privileges be preserved and they be permitted to do accordingly."[32]

The decrees thus far noticed concern Roman citizens. It is best to indicate the essentially religious nature of the *privilegia* granted to the citizens of Rome by contrasting it with the fundamentally political basis of the *privilegia* granted to members of the Jewish nation or *peregrini*. The political basis appears in the following decree which is usually dated somewhere between 113 and 105 B.C. and is concerned with a decision of the Senate elicited by ambassadors of the Jewish nation.

"The magistrates of the Laodiceans to Caius Rubilius . . . Sopater the ambassador of Hyrcanus the high priest hath delivered us an epistle from thee whereby he lets us know that certain ambassadors were come from Hyrcanus, the high priest of the Jews and brought an epistle written *concerning their nation*[33] wherein they desire that the Jews may be allowed to observe their Sabbaths and other sacred rites according to the laws of their forefathers and that they may be under no command because *they are our friends and allies*."[34][35]

The decrees hitherto cited are from the Republican era. The following is from the period of Cæsar, and was issued by a Roman magistrate, whose name, however, the text does not reveal. This decree also grants the Jewish *nation* certain privileges connected with religion and then it compares the situation of the Jews in the town to which the decree is addressed with their position " even at Rome " where they have enjoyed religious privileges by the gift of Cæsar. It will be noted, moreover, that the decreeing magistrate when he refers to the Jews of Parium always speaks of " their national customs . . . as friends and allies " as if this were a set formula. But he omits these formulæ when he speaks of the Jews at Rome. The decree's substance follows :

" . . . to the magistrates, to the council and the people of the Parians, greetings. The Jews of Delos(?) have come to see me with some Jews living amongst you and in the presence of your envoys have explained to me that you interdicted by decree the practice of their national customs and religion. It does not please me that such decrees are issued against our *friends and allies*,[36] forbidding them to live according to their customs, to collect money for common banquets and ceremonies, even when at Rome they are not prevented from doing so. For when Caius Cæsar, our commander-in-chief, interdicted by decree the formation of *associations*[37] at Rome, the Jews are the only ones whom he has not forbidden *to collect money or to make common banquets*.[38] In the same way I, also, interdicting all other associations, authorize the Jews alone to live according to their *national customs and laws*, and to assemble in banquets. As for you, if you have passed any decree against our *friends and allies*, it is time that you revoked it because of the services they have rendered us and their dispositions in our favour."[39]

Besides the features in this decree to which we alluded (which give some clue to the dualistic character of the Jewish *privilegia*) there is the additional fact that the decree envisages the organization of the Jews both in the East and the West as based on associations or *collegia*.

The distinction which is suggested in the *Acta* just cited is not generally maintained by other decrees of the Emperors.[40] Thus all the Augustan decrees are apparently issued to the Jews in the Greek cities and are therefore of a political type.[41] We possess no decrees of his in favour of Jews in the West. Similarly the decrees of the Emperor Claudius are addressed to the Jews of Egypt and to the Jews of the rest of the Empire (probably to the Jews of the East though this is not clear).[42] Is is significant that a special bequest characterizes each grant. One decree is addressed to the " Jewish nation of Alexandria " while another is designed to extend the decree to all the Jews of the Empire and is accordingly addressed in general terms to all Jews. There is every likelihood that this grant also is national in its nature, though it is conceivable that it was intended to regulate the two groups at the same time; that is, to confirm the privileges of the Jewish Roman citizens in the West and those of the *peregrini* in the East, which were identical. However, it is clear from the special grant to Alexandria that the Romans were also in the habit of dealing with each community separately, and this is strongly suggested by the evidence from the earlier *Acta*.

IV. Sources of confusion : religion and nation.

Notwithstanding the legal distinction it was natural for the average person to confuse Judaism and Jewish nationality because of their more obvious geographical connection. The religion embodied in the *religio licita* and the religion of the Jewish nation were after all identical in point of fact and different only in point of law. Furthermore, in ordinary parlance it might even be regarded as pedantic on the part of a person to distinguish properly between a licensed religion and a national religion on which it was historically based.[43] It is only on this supposition that one can account for the confusion in the two terminologies of which Philo is guilty.[44]

Aside from the possible confusion involved in the ancient use of the term, a prolific source of misunderstanding to modern students comes from the use of terms in a special sense. An interesting illustration of this differentiation may be cited. Suetonius, in speaking of the expulsion of the Jews by Tiberius, refines his terms : " Reliquos gentis eiusdem vel similia sectantes urbe summovit, sub pœna perpetuæ servitutis nisi obtemperassent."[45] Here Suetonius is very obviously contrasting Jews by race and Jews by profession. His use of the term *gens* is ethnic then.[46]

There is nothing in the use of such terms as *ethnos* or *gens* that is necessarily in conflict with a *religio licita*. Tertullian describes Judaism rightly as an " insignissima religio, certe licita " and there is nothing in our evidence which can be said to gainsay the truth of this declaration.[42]

V. *Fiscus Judaicus.*

But Mommsen was considerably exercised over the *Fiscus Judaicus*.[47] After predicating a confessional basis for the Jewish *privilegia* after 70, he found himself confronted with the evidence of the *didrachma*, to all appearances a levy on the Jewish " nation " at large. After attempting to prove that it was really a tax on the religion and not on the race or " nation " Mommsen, as we have pointed out, altered his position to the extent of accepting a hereditary basis for the Jewish *religio licita*, and thus, in the eyes of Juster, vitiating his thesis.[48]

Was the didrachma imposed on the nation?

The question which troubled Mommsen can with greater reason trouble a view that the *religio licita* preceded the year 70. The *didrachma* was imposed after the fall of Jerusalem as a sort of tribute on the conquered Jews and was therefore evidently of a political or national character. If it was this, and affected all the Jews in the Empire (East and West) as it probably did, there is a presumption that the basis of the Jewish position throughout the Empire was political and national previous to 70. This conclusion follows from the premises. Both premises and conclusions are fallible, however. In the first place, the strictly political connection between the *Fiscus* and the fall of Jerusalem is open to question and secondly, the motive of its imposition as far as we know from the evidence was opportunist and fiscal more than anything else. But, most important of all, is the fact that the *didrachma* was always regarded as irregular and extortionate. This feeling is reflected in the lines of Martial cited in a preceding note. The illegality of the tax is almost implied in the legend on coins of the reign of Nerva, " Fisci Judaici calumnia sublata."[49] Furthermore, there is really no more reason to attach a universal or non-national significance to the *didrachma* than to the imposts that had been levied previously in Palestine. Pompey had imposed such a tax in 63 B.C., and after the exile of Archelaus an annual tax, the *tributum capitis* was collected from all Jews.[50]

The Roman Emperors were greatly in need of funds at all times. In response to this need the *Fisci Alexandrinus* and *Asiaticus* were established. It was in response to the same need that Vespasian, whose avarice was notorious, exploited the Jews. Their revolt in A.D. 66–70 gave him his opportunity.[51] The Jews had, from time immemorial, possessed a hallowed institution, the Temple Tithe. Every Jewish community in the Diaspora sent its annual money offering to the Temple at Jerusalem and this sum mounted to a considerable sum as the Jewish position in the Diaspora became more firmly entrenched. When the Temple was destroyed in A.D. 70 this temple tithe had no legitimate destination. What was to be done with it? The emperor answered the question by confiscating it as a public fund which had lost its original *raison d'être* and was therefore the property of the state. In order to legalize the act, however, the board administering the fund was designated as *Fiscus Judaicus*. The *didrachma*, a sort of tax on the Jewish cult administered by the board, was diverted to the treasury of Jupiter Capitolinus. In other words the legalization followed the act, which in turn had been dictated by motives of expediency. Suetonius in the passage cited lends colour to this view of the tax as a mere financial boon to the state when he reveals to what lengths Domitian was prepared to go, to utilize the *didrachma* in his effort to raise money for himself.

The didrachma not imposed on the nation.

Having confiscated the original sum the emperor was loath to neglect for the future such a valuable source of income. The *didrachma* was, therefore, after the analogy of the old Temple Tithe, which provided the precedent, made an annual tax. But on whom was this tax to be imposed? Only on members of the Jewish nation which had just been conquered, or on all Jews regardless of their political status? The emperors found a speedy solution to this problem also. They made the tax obligatory on *all Jewish communities which had formerly* sent the Temple Tithe to Jerusalem; this affected all Jewish communities in the West which had formerly been in the habit of sending tithes but did not affect the race as such. The emperors, by thus making this exaction a sort of successor (for the purposes of taxation) to the Temple Tithe, to which even Roman citizens had been in the habit of contributing, removed the whole matter from the sphere of political significance and placed it on a purely fiscal basis.

There is no doubt that Romans had always looked askance at the spectacle of Roman citizens sending a sort of annual tribute to a foreign temple. It was for this reason, probably, and because there was a strong feeling that money should not be permitted to leave the peninsula in large amounts, that Cicero in 63 B.C. had forbidden the exportation of the Jewish Temple Tithe.[52] But the emperors had tolerated the practice as not involving any fundamental violation of Roman citizenship. When the Temple was destroyed, this source of misunderstanding was removed. There is nothing, at any rate, in the Temple Tithe or the *Fiscus Judaicus* which implies a national basis for the Jewish *privilegia* of the West, nor anything which is incompatible with the character of Judaism as a *religio licita* in Italy and the western parts of the empire.

VI. Meaning of term religio licita.

But what did the *religio licita* involve ? Juster asks and answers this question in connection with Mommsen's view expressed in the *Strafrecht*, that after 70 Judaism was a hereditary licensed cult. Juster regards the notion of heredity (or for that matter any limitation) as incompatible with the status of a *religio licita*.[53] A *religio licita* should have been able to admit within its fold all who applied for entrance, if it were an authorized cult of the Roman state, and if it was unable to do so, as Judaism was unable to admit proselytes, it was not a *religio licita*. Nor could it have been a *religio licita* if its activities were in any way limited, as those of the Jews were. This is to state the situation unsatisfactorily. Juster in this case fails to distinguish between the general legal position of the *religio licita* and its executive regulation. The first might conceivably be constant, the second was certainly variable and subject to the whims of the enforcing or legislating official. The policy of the state toward the Isis cult is an example in point.[54] This cult existed in Rome as far back as Sulla's time without the cognizance of the government.[55] But in 58 the cult was suppressed at Rome by the consul.[56] In 53 [57] and in 50[58] the cult was again excluded from the city. After these repressive measures the cult received a respite when the triumvirs in 43 B.C. dedicated a temple of Isis and Serapis.[59] The cult thereafter enjoyed a certain amount of toleration as an authorized religion.[60]   Augustus, however, in conformance with his programme of religious reform excluded the cult from the *pomerium*, though he protected it in other ways as Dio describes : " As for religious matters he did not allow the Egyptian rites to be celebrated inside the *pomerium*, but made provision for the temples ; those which had been built by private individuals he ordered their sons and descendants, if any survived, to repair and the rest he restored himself."[61]   Augustus' policy in regard to this cult was, therefore, a mixture of recognition and limitation. Despite the apparant recognition it enjoyed at the hands of Augustus, Agrippa did not hesitate to exclude the sect from the suburbs.[62]   Tiberius in his turn drove the cult from the city.[63]   Notwithstanding these reverses we find it again flourishing and even conducting a temple on the capitol in the time of Nero.[64] Such a stage of recognition had the worship attained that when in the time of Titus its Temple was burnt down an Iseum was built by Domitian.[65]   It is clear then that the governmental policy toward the foreign cults, which were often admitted by law, was essentially the policy of individual magistrates or emperors, and this differed.   The same thing was true of Judaism ; the existence of limitations on its observance, limitations depending on individuals, does not necessarily disprove that it was licensed.   One must bear in mind then the two-fold complexion of the problem connected with the existence of a cult like Judaism—in the first place its position in law and in the second its position in fact (laws could be changed).   Its position in law might be unquestioned, it might even in theory possess the right to proselytize, for we know that Judaism attracted a number of converts to its fold in the first centuries.

In fact, however, it is conceivable that emperors would try to limit this privilege, as many of them (though by no means all) did. The fact that there was no law in the empire that dealt with proselytism lends some colour to the view that Judaism had a *right* to proselytize. Curiously enough when an emperor did adopt measures against proselytism his method was roundabout. The culprit was accused of "Atheism," that is, failure to comply with the state cult, but not accused of the positive practice of Judaism,[66]

Danger of excessive precision in use of term.

It is equally clear from the preceding considerations that there was no precision in the Roman notion of a *religio licita*, precision in the sense in which Juster understands the word. It is interesting to note the restrictions and limitations that were imposed on some of the licensed cults of Rome. Not all of them were in the first place admitted within the *pomerium*, the sacred boundary of the old city of Rome. To the latter honour only the *dii indigetes* or native Italian gods were entitled.[67] The *dii novensiles*, though official gods of the state, were not admitted within the *pomerium* unless they were identified and merged with, the native gods, the *indigetes*. The latter contingency occurred in the time of the Second Punic War when the Phrygian goddess Cybele was brought to Italy and identified with the *Roman Magna Mater*, thus gaining access to the sacred enclosure.[68] Judaism, however, never had its synagogues admitted within the *pomerium*.[69] *Cybele*, like Judaism, demanded a closed cult in many ways. Dionysius is authority for the statement that Roman citizens even in the time of Augustus were forbidden to take a leading part in the ceremonies of the Great Mother and that the priesthood was restricted to Phrygians.[70] In other words, here we have an undoubtedly licensed and consecrated religion of the state subjected to various restrictions as regards membership and conduct, restrictions of the same type as surrounded the practice of Judaism in the empire.

VII. *Christianity, basis of persecution, religious as well as national.*

The essentially religious basis of the Jewish position in the Latin world is revealed by its connection with Christianity, an offspring that unfortunately failed to secure the necessary toleration and was soon made the object of systematic persecution. In its infancy, however, Christianity drew some measure of security from its relations with Judaism or as Tertullian puts it, " quasi sub umbraculo insignissimæ religionis."[71] Juster draws from this evidence the conclusion that it was because Christians passed as members of the Jewish nation that they were originally tolerated, and that the institution of persecution of Christianity marks the first evidence of the cognizance by the government of religious differences.[72] Juster himself admits that situation a paradox in which a government which was only aware of a *nation* should also take account of religious differences in that nation and proscribe one sect in it, should in other words make the basis of its recognition *religion* and not *nation*.[73] It would seem to be simpler, in the light of the fact that the Roman government did take account subsequently of religious differences to the extent of undertaking a programme of persecution against Christians, to assume that in the first place also it was both the Jewish religion and the nation under whose wing Christians enjoyed toleration ; assume, in other words, that Judaism as a *religio licita* would offer a haven of refuge for some Christians. Juster also brings into line the manœuvres of the Christian apologists who were ever trying to prove that Christians were the true Jews, Christianity the true Judaism. According to him they were trying to obtain for themselves the protection accorded to the Jewish *nation*. But it was the protection of the *religio licita*, as well as of the *natio*, for which the Christians were striving. At any rate the very fact that the Roman government declared Christianity a *religio illicita* after a temporary relationship with Judaism clearly indicates the religious basis of some of the latter's privileges.

Conclusion.

In general, then, Judaism was a *religio licita* in those parts of the West where Roman citizens were found in sufficient numbers to warrant the Roman government's taking special account of them as communities. But it was a *religio licita*, in all probability, with heredity as a condition of membership. In the East the *natio* was and continued to be the basis of Jewish privileges during the first two centuries. When the Emperor Caracalla admitted all Jews to citizenship and public office in the third century, then, and not till then did the distinction between the West and East disappear.[74]

NOTES

(1) It is probable that even at Alexandria the Jews were, as a group, still *peregrini*. Despite Josephus' affirmations (*Contra Apionem*, II, 4; *Wars (Bel. Jud.)*, II, 2, 8, 7; *Ant.*, XIV, 5, 2), it appears from the Claudian edict in Bell's work (*Jews and Christians at Alexandria*), that the Jews were always referred to on terms separate from those of the Greeks, and that Josephus' phrase that the Jews were put "on a footing of equality" by Alexander does not mean "on a similar footing." This distinction is Kenyon's, expressed in his article "Jews in Roman Egypt," *Edinburgh Review*, 242: 32–47 (1925). It is followed by Bell in the work cited, by H. S. Jones in an article in *Journal of Roman Studies*, 16: 17–35 (1926) and by other students (Reinach, Jouguet).

(2) Mommsen, *Provinces of Roman Empire*, II, Chap. "Judaea and Jews," *passim*. In fact, some students are not even aware of the possibility of such a distinction. See for example article "Ancient Rome and Religious Cults," by E. T. Merrill, *Classical Journal*, 1920, 196–215. The latter, p. 211, identifies a *religio licita* with a national religion. So also Waltzing, in his edition of Tertullian's *Apologeticus*, Louvain, 1910, p. 125, makes a *religio licita* depend on its national character. It was because, according to him, Christianity was not such a national religion that it was not tolerated. Needless to say that such a view runs counter to what we have said. Only a non-foreign religion was open to Roman citizens and as long as Judaism remained a foreign cult it was closed to citizens.

(4) For Mommsen's view see his own statement in *Hist. Zeitsch.*, LXIV, 1890, pp. 389–429. Hereafter any view ascribed to Mommsen, unless otherwise documented, goes back to this article.

(5) According to Van Groningen, *Aegyptus*, VII, 1926, 189–202, the inhabitants of Egypt became *dediticii* as a result of Octavian's conquest, and this accounts for its exceptional position later by the side of other provinces. Usually, however, only the actual combatants became public slaves. Even this rule was mitigated and compromises arranged

such as the one involving the Anagni. Livy 9, 43, 24 :
"Anagnis quique arma Romanis intulerant civitas sine
suffragii latione data, concilia conubiaque adempta et magis-
tratibus praeterquam sacrorum curatione interdictum." On
the whole Mommsen's theory does not square with the facts.

(6) It is simply incompatible with the Roman notion of citizenship.
Juster, II, 15 ff. Furthermore, Vespasian and Titus were
aided by Jewish contingents led by several members of the
Herod dynasty, and numbered among their advisers Jews
like Josephus and Berenice.

(7) Juster, I, p. 419, note, points out that the Senate continues to
exist in Jewish communities after A.D. 70.

(8) Open to all, according to Juster. See *infra*, however.

(9) *Historische Zeitschrift, loc. cit.*, p. 415—cf., however, *Strafrecht*,
Leipzig, 1899, pp. 537-546.

(10) Jos., *Bel. Jud.*, VII, 6, 6.

(11) Suetonius, *Domitian*, 9, 12. Cf. also Martial, VII, 55, 7 :
    " Sed quae de Solymis venit perustis
      Damnatum modo mentulam tributis."
    Martial, VII, 82 :
    " Menophili penem tam gravis fibula vestit
      Ut sit comoedis omnibus una satis.
      Hung ego credideram nam saepe lavamur in unum
      Sollicitum voci parcere, Flacce, suae
      Dum ludit media populo spectante, palaestra,
      Delapsa est misero fibula : verpus erat."
    For an interpretation of these passages see Leclercq, art.
    " Domitien," *Dict. d'arch. chrét.*, fasc. XL, col. 1390.

(12) Hardy, E. G., *The Roman Government and Christianity*, p. 31.
    Cf. S. Gsell, *Essai sur le régne de l'empéreur Domitien*, Paris,
    1894, p. 287.

(13) *Röm. Strafrecht*, pp. 537 ff.

(14) Dio Cassius, for example (Epitome of Xiphilinus LXVII, 14),
    mentions the prosecution and death of the consul, Flavius

Clemens, on the charge of " Atheism," for practising Judaism. *Textes d'auteurs grecs et romains relatifs au Judaisme*, Ed. T. Reinach, Paris, 1895, p. 195.

(15) It may refer to a group of Jews who had been compelled by the persecutions of Hadrian to forego their religion.

(16) See chapter III of present work.

(17) Juster, II, p. 15 ff. Leclercq, art. " Judaisme." *Dict. d'arch. chrét.*, fasc. LXXX, cols. 64, 65.

(18) Juster, I, 418, note 1 : " Noter que les Juifs ne mentionment jamais sur leurs tombes la communauté dont ils ont fait partie ; mais ils mettent plutôt qu'ils sont Juifs, c'est a dire membres de la nation juive.'

(19) For mention of synagogue see Muller-Bees, *op. cit.*, nos. 2, 3, 14, 25, 106, 107, 108, 109, 110, 111, 174, 175. For mention of race or religion see no. 117 (Ἰουλινὸς Ἐβρεος), 118, 122 (Ἐβραιος), 176 (Ἰουδέα). It is worth noting that the words Hebrew and Jew are usually attached to those whose *origo* was some city other than Rome. The *origo* of residents of Rome is not given. (See Reinach, *Rev. des ét Juives*, t. LXXI, p. 114). The term Hebrew appears to have been applied to former Palestinians. It is difficult to say whether any special significance attached to the use of these terms.

(20) *Les Juifs*, I, 154. See Niese, *Hermes*, XI, 466, who regards them as collected by Nicolaus and Ritschl, *Phil. Mus.*, XXVIII, 599, in an opposite sense. See also art. " Josephus," *Jewish Encyclopedia*, vol. VII, p. 274 ; art. " Josephus," in Pauly-Wissowa, *Réalencyclopädie*.

(21) It is a commonplace that Josephus sometimes cites data that appear to be contradictory. Destinon concluded that Josephus reproduced conflicting and often inaccurate sources without understanding them. Taeubler, *Hermes*, 1916, p. 211–232, points out that these questionable data occur only in the XIIth and XIIIth books and are probably based on some anonymous source. The *Acta* cited above are from book XIV. Nevertheless, in view of the jumbled character of some

of Josephus' testimony, it is " safer to study these documents as fragments rather than in their context." (M. Ginsburg, *Rome et la Judeé*, p. 86).

[22] Juster, *op. cit.*, I, p. 142. *Josephi Opera*, Ed. Niese, Berlin, 1890–1900.

[23] πολίτας Ῥωμάιων.

[24] ἱερὰ Ἰουδαικα ἔχοντας

[25] δεισιδαιμονίας ἕνεχα.

[26] *Ant.*, XIV, 10, 13.

[27] εἰ τινες εἰσιν Ἰουδαῖοι πολῖπαι Ῥωμαιων.

[28] δεισιδαιμονίας ἕνεχα

[29] *Ant.*, XIV, 10, 14.

[30] Reading πολῖται ἡμέτεροι with Niese. There is one reading which would involve Jews enjoying citizenship of Sardis. But the intervention of the Roman proquaestor is understandable in the former case. See the note to the French translation of the *Antiquities* edited by Reinach, *Oeuvres complètes de Flavius Josèphe traduites en francais*, 4V., Paris, 1904, III, 248, note 3.

[31] ἐπέδει ξαι αὐτοὺς συνοδον ἔχειν ἰδίαν.

[32] *Ant.*, XIV, 10, 17.

[33] περι του ἔθνους ἀυτῶν.

[34] δία το φίλους αὐτοις ἡμετέρους ἔιναι και συμμάχους.

[35] *Ant.*, XIV, 10, 20.

[36] κατὰ τᾶν ἡμετέρων φίλων και συμμάχων.

[37] θιασους.

[38] οὔτε χρήματα συνεισφέρειν οὔτε σύν δει πνα ποεῖν.

[39] *Ant.*, XIV, 10, 8.

[40] The formulae employed in the *Acta* of the Republican period, however, seem to disappear. Are we to assume that some method was designed in the Republican and Caesarian periods, for distinguishing between the two classes of Jews that fell into desuetude later ? Our evidence is not decisive.

(41) *Ant.*, XVI, 6, 3-7.

(42) *Ant.*, XIX, 5, 5 ; XIX, 5, 3 XIX, 6, 3.

(43) Even in an enlightened age like ours there is considerable confusion in the use of terms connected with nationality. Thus " French " is often used for " French-American."

(44) *Leg. Ad. Caium*, 23. Philo speaks of Augustus' toleration of the Jews at Rome as based on his " regard for Judaea." But Philo's discussion is in the nature of a religious sermon, not a legal disquisition and one can understand why he should try to laud the national achievements of the Jews. H. Stuart Jones (*loc. cit.*, " Claudius and the Jewish Question at Alexandria," *J. Rom. Studies*, 16 : 17-35), has remarked with a touch of whimsicality that if Philo had given us one more good historical treatise instead of his twenty-odd allegorical treatises we should be very thankful.

(45) *Tiberius*, 36.

(46) A similar instance occurs in Dio Cassius (*Roman History*, 17) :

" Ἡ δέ ἐπίχλησις αὑτη ἐχείνος μευ ουχοιδ ὅθεν ἦρξατο γενεσθαι φέρει δέ χαι ἐπί τους ἄλλους ἀνθρωπους ὅσοι τὰ νόμιμα αὐτῶν, χαίπερ ἀλλοεθνεῖς ὄντες ζηλοῦσι. "

ἀλλοεθνείζ here means " of another race," not " of another nation."

(46)ª Tertullian, *Apologeticus*, XXI.

(47) The term *Fiscus Judaicus* did not, as Juster, I, p. 283, believes, refer to the tax itself but to the board administering it. See M. Ginsburg, *Jewish Quarterly Review*, 1931, p. 285.

(48) Mommsen, *Hist. Zeit.*, 1890, p. 424, 425.

(49) Cohen, *Nerva*, no. 51.

(50) For Pompey's tax see Jos., *Bel. Jud.*, I, 7, 6. For both see L. Goldschmidt, *Rev. des et. juives*, tome 34, 1897, pp. 192, 194.

(51) See M. Ginsburg, *Jewish Quarterly Review*, 1931, p. 285. Hirschfeld, *Die Kais. Verwaltungsbeamt. bis auf Diocletian*, p. 14, shows the resemblance of the three *fisci*.

(52) *Pro Flacco*, 67.

(53) *Les Juifs*, I, 416.

(54) Burel, Joseph, " Isis et Isiaques sons l'empire romain," *Etude de critique et de philosophie religieuse*, Paris, 1911, pp. 5 ff.

(55) Apul., *Met.*, XI, 17: " Coetu pastophorum quod sacrosancti collegii nomen est . . . collegium vetustissimum et sub illis Sullae temporibus conditum." Cf. Diodorus Siculus, I, 29.

(56) Tertullian, *Apol.*, 6.

(57) Dio Cas., XI, 47.

(58) Val. Max., I, 3, 3.

(59) Dio Cas., XLVII, 15.

(60) Arnob., II, 73 : " Quid vos, Aegyptiaca numina quibus Serapis atque Isis est nomen, non post Pisonem et Gabinium consules in numerum vestrorum rettulistis deorum."

(61) Dio Cas., LIII, 2.   A number of factors contributed to the recognition of the cults (Hardy, *Christianity and Roman Government*, p. 13) : (1) public dangers like the plague induced the Romans to hunt for new divinities (Dionysius X, 53 ; Livy IV, 30, and XXV, 1) ; (2) the earlier political character of the Roman religion made it a religion of an oligarchy ; the lower classes had to hunt elsewhere for their religion.

(62) Dio. Cas., LIV, 6.

(63) Suetonius, *Tiberius*.

(64) Tac., *Hist.*, III, 74.

(65) Eutropius, 7, 23.

(66) Cf. passage cited above in Dio Cas., LXVII, 14 ; and also Suetonius, *Domitian*, 2, 12. See also Juster, I, 256–258.

(67) Arnobius, III, 38.

(68) Marquardt, *Le Culte*, I, 10 ff.

(69) This is the safest conjecture, though it is not impossible that one at least of the synagogues known to us may have been within the *pomoerium* before the time of Diocletian.

[70] Passage cited above, II, 19.

[71] *Apol.*, XXI.

[72] The real basis of the Christian persecution is still a question *sub judice*. There are two or three views on the subject. Mommsen held that there was no general law passed against the Christians but that they were suppressed by the *ius coercitionis* of the individual magistrate. The famous letters of Pliny and Trajan give Mommsen some warrant for his view which, besides, explains (1) The peculiar punishments meted out to Christians, punishments unknown to Roman penal law. (2) The absence of a regular trial procedure. (3) The fact that there was no regular charge against Christians except that they were Christians. For a summary of this view see Mommsen's *Strafrecht*. The other view, which is by no means untenable, is that a general law was at bottom of the persecutions. For this view see Paul Allard's *Histoire des Persécutions*, Paris, 1903, *passim*. C. Callewart, in an article, " Les Premiers Chrétiens furent-ils persécutés par édits generaux ou par mesures de police ? " (*Revue de histoire ecclesiastique*, II, 1901, III, 1902), has given a lengthy refutation of Mommsen's view. But the question is still unsolved, and as long as there will be polemicists and no definite evidence one way or another, the controversy bids fair to rage. See Chapter II of present work for fuller discussion.

[73] Juster, I, 423, note.

[74] See note [9b] in first chapter.

CHAPTER SIX

THE SYNAGOGUES AND THE *COLLEGIA*[1]

THE basis of the *religio licita* was the *collegium licitum*. When a group of individuals organized an association with some religious or practical end in view and obtained the necessary authorization of the state they then constituted a *collegium licitum*.[2]

It is not strange then that the Jewish synagogue or community should find it best for legal purposes to become an association with certain rights and privileges.[3] Particularly in the West where the nation was not the foundation of the Jewish recognition, the adaptation was almost inevitable since Roman law took no other account of a group unless it was organized as an association.[4] In the East also the Jewish community took the typical form of *collegium*, but whether it there enjoyed the full rights of *collegia* is doubtful, as we shall presently indicate. At any rate in the East it was the *natio* which provided the basis of the recognition of the Jewish community and the consequent difference in political status alone could account for differences in the rights and status of the respective *collegia*. But that both the communities of East and West possessed this typical organization of *collegia* our evidence does not permit us to doubt.

I. Terms employed in descriptions of synagogues and collegia.

A single legal text refers to the Jewish communities at Rome and Parium as θιασοι or *collegia*.[5] Another text implies that the Jewish community at Alexandria was regarded as an association.[6] It is when Agrippa, arguing the cause of his fellow Jews before Caligula, recalls that if Augustus countenanced the Jewish associations it was because they were schools of temperance and of justice ; if the prefect of Egypt, Flaccus, interdicted, the other religious corporations (εταιρειαι και συνοδοι) it was because their festivities often interfered with the public peace.

These texts seem to be sufficiently explicit in themselves, but the paucity of additional evidence identifying the Jewish communities with *collegia* has inspired doubts in the minds of some scholars as to their complete reliability. On this basis, Juster argues against the identification of synagogues with *collegia*.[7] The fact that the Jewish community was always referred to collectively as *universitas* or *corpus*, or by some similar designation suggests to him that the Jewish community or synagogue was not commonly regarded as a *collegium*. As a matter of fact a diversity of names was used in designating corporations. A glance through the section in the *Corpus* dealing with the *collegia* will confirm this remark. Among the terms used for corporation are *Sodalicium, Sodalitas, Societas*[8] (an association formed between people for a fixed time). Another term widely used is *Ordo*, which was applied to those who had the government of a community ; in this case *ordo* commonly replaced *collegium*. Still more common is the use of the term *corpus* (συστημα). This term connoted that the college was " authorized, recognized as a public organism and, consequently endowed with the rights which constitute its civil personality."[9]   The lack, therefore, of evidence for the use of such familiar terms as *collegium* or θιασοι is by no means to be construed as a vital defect.[10]

II. *Resemblances between synagogues and collegia.*

In the text cited above Josephus also describes the special features common to all *collegia*, features which Cæsar guaranteed to the Jewish associations at Rome and which the magistrate in the decree is prepared to grant to the Jews of Parium[11] These privileges are the possession of a treasury and the gathering for banquets.   These characteristics of *collegia* are mentioned in numerous texts and inscriptions and appear to be fundamental to the legal notion of the *collegium*.[12] The Jewish communities always had the right to a common treasury and permission to unite for common banquets, and in these particulars certainly conformed to the position of *collegia*.

Tertullian has given us an excellent picture of the life of a Christian *corpus* in Africa.[13]   He enumerates a number of features of its life, which are apparently common to all *collegia*.   These include the election of officers, a treasury replenished by monthly assessments, meals in common, provisions for funerals and a number of other activities more or less related.[14]   The activities of the Jewish community or synagogue paralleled all these activities, and included many more.   It, too, made provision for the election of officers, for regular assessments, for meals in common, for the burial of members

132

and a host of other duties. Like other *collegia*, it possessed its general assemblies.[15] Thus far for certain external similarities ; we shall return to special aspects of this resemblance again in another connection.

III. *Differences between the Jewish associations of the East and the West revealed by the question of right of receiving bequests.*

But the most significant of all these resemblances was that the Jewish communities possessed a juridical personality. This was implied in the recognition of the Jewish right to maintain community treasuries and levy assessments on members. This juridical personality involved in turn a number of other distinct rights. It implied that the Jewish community had the right to purchase and maintain land, to sell, and to contract obligations, to receive donations and give donations, the right to send legations to the emperor, and finally to receive legacies, after the reign of Marcus Aurelius.[16]

It is the question of receiving legacies that in our opinion reveals the essential differences between the Jewish *collegia* in the West, particularly in Italy, and those in the East.

If the Jewish communities had possessed a legal personality like the *collegia*, one would have expected them, after the measure of Marcus Aurelius which gave the right of receiving legacies to *collegia licita*, to share in this grant.[17] What is our surprise then, to find a rescript of Caracalla forbidding the Jewish Universitas of Antioch to accept a legacy left by a certain Cornelia Salvia.[18] Numerous explanations have been made of this anomaly, for anomaly it is in the light of the known legal personality of the Jewish community previous to this event. Some have taken it to mean that the Jewish community enjoyed some legal rights, but not all, and that among the rights it did not enjoy was that of receiving legacies. This explanation is legally inadmissible since Roman law knew little distinction between full civil personality and quasi-civil personality. Another explanation offered is that the bequest to the Jewish community came from a non-Jew and was, for this reason, refused. This explanation is also inadequate. First, we do not know that Cornelia Salvia was not Jewish, and we cannot argue from her name that she was. A second consideration lies in the fact that the only other instance we have of a bequest left by a Jew after the law of Caracalla is a legacy left to a society of Jewish artisans at Hierapolis ;[19] the implication, according to Juster, being that the donor unable to leave the money to the Jewish community left it to the corporation of Jewish artisans. Juster's own conclusion is that we are confronted in the rescript of Caracalla with a special disposition, the circumstances of which are unknown.[20] However, there is a simpler explanation for it all.[21]

In essence it is this. The law passed in Marcus Aurelius' reign granting *collegia licita* the right to receive legacies applied only to Italy.[22] Jewish communities in Italy would therefore fall under its provisions which, however, would not extend to Jewish communities outside the peninsula. This explanation is based on Cuq's view that the law of Marcus Aurelius had a limited sphere of application. The foregoing solution, if correct, lends colour to the dualistic hypothesis we have ried to develop in this work. This case of the special favour granted to Italy by Marcus Aurelius and the consequent debasement of the provinces (forces which operated with even greater vigour at the opening of the Empire) gives a valuable clue to the influences which were working to keep the status of the Jews in the West distinct from that of the Jews in the East. The differences in the legal status of their associations was probably one of degree : the Jewish *collegia* in the East because of their lesser position did not enjoy all the advantages of those in the West. What their precise legal character was or what else constituted the difference in status we are unfortunately not able to say. That a difference existed in many respects everything leads us to believe. We know, for example, that the Jewish community in the East by virtue of its political position (as part of the Jewish nation) exercised a much greater civil and even criminal jurisdiction over its members than did the Jewish community in the West. The Jewish community at Alexandria may even have had the theoretical right to put one of its members to death.[23] The Jewish community in the West, however, enjoyed only a limited jurisdiction, a jurisdiction which was really of the type exercised by some *collegia* (though more complicated).[24] The advantages, on the other hand which the Jews of the West enjoyed were the advantages in the way of political security and influence which Roman citizenship brought its recipients.[25] Such an advantage is predicated in the law of Marcus Aurelius which granted associations in Italy the right to receive legacies.

IV. Objections to the identification of collegia and synagogues.

But the identification of the synagogues with the *collegia* has been challenged on a number of grounds.

It has been urged that the points of difference between the two are so conspicuous and numerous as to preclude the possibility of their having belonged to one legal category. Juster does not hesitate to regard the Synagogue as an institution *sui generis*, distinct from the large body of associations in the Empire.[26]

(1) *Submission of synagogues to a central authority.*

In the first place, Juster asserts that the Jewish communities differed from the *collegia* in the fact that the former were members of the Jewish nation and, unlike the *collegia*, owed allegiance to one central authority. In reply we will remain content with reaffirming that the Jewish communities in the West did not form part of the Jewish nation (legally speaking) and that their subjection to the central Jewish authority was no more than a moral or spiritual one.[27] Furthermore, even for the Jewish communities in the East it is doubtful whether their adherence to a political or national system would constitute a fundamental breach of their legal position as associations, for the latter, as we shall point out, exhibited many forms.[28]

(2) *Synagogues commonly have no "statutes."*

Another difference Juster points to as conclusive is that while the *collegium* possessed its own " statutes," which when approved by the state formed the basis of its recognition as a licensed association, the Jewish community possessed nothing similar ; the only statute it recognized was the law of Moses.[29] Even assuming this to be a difference (and we are unable to do so for we shall presently bring in evidence cited by Juster himself that the Jewish community did possess its own statutes[30]) one cannot regard it as conclusive. The Jewish communities happened to possess one instead of many statutes. In fact the government might encourage such unanimity as simplifying the problem of supervision and regulation of the individual communities. The same thing might be true of the absence of a special grant of *coire licet* in the case of the Jewish community.[31] Here also the government instead of bothering to approve the statute of each new community might find it more convenient simply to licence the cult in the first place and approve the simple statute (Law of Moses) which formed the uniform basis of the Jewish associations everywhere. We shall return to the question of the lack of *coire licet* presently. But it is evident that while differences might exist between the Jewish communities and the *collegia* as a whole these differences are capable of a simple explanation and need not in themselves interfere with the assimilation of synagogues to *collegia*. Thus far for some *a priori* considerations.

Juster enumerates, more definitely, a number of arguments against the identification of the synagogue with the *collegium* that appear conclusive to him when taken together.[32] We shall list them here and then attempt briefly to answer them : 1. Unlike any *collegia*, membership in the Synagogues was acquired by birth. 2. The non-Jew could not become a member. The Roman law, according to Juster, did not recognize *collegia licita*, to which only members of a single race were eligible. 3. The functions of the community were more complex than those of the *collegia* ; and 4. (*a*) the Jewish community itself was a combination of synagogues which formed one great " city." The *collegium*, according to Juster, was a unit by itself and not connected with a large number of other units in a single organization. (*b*) From another angle also the Jewish community was a much larger organization than the ordinary *collegium* ; the Jewish community was a sort of city within a city. 5. The Jewish synagogue possessed no statutes like those of the *collegia*. 6. The Jews possessed associations of artizans which were *collegia licita* ; it was because the community or synagogue was not a *collegium licitum* that there was not in this case a violation of the rule in the Digest which forbade membership in two *collegia* at the same time.[33] 7. The Jewish synagogue did not need the special grant of *coire licet* as the *collegium licitum* did. We shall take up these objections and in presenting our rebuttal attempt to envisage for the reader the synagogue in the actual role of *collegium licitum*.

(3) *Absence of coire licet in case of synagogues.*

As regards the *coire licet* it is clear that a number of categories of *collegia* were not obliged by law to conform to it. Under the Republic, in the first place, once a cult was authorized by the government, the latter did not have to intervene to authorize the colleges which were dedicated to it.[34] Once, therefore, the Jewish religion was *licita*, its synagogues automatically enjoyed the rights of *collegia licita*.

Under the empire the rules relating to the organization of *collegia* were made more stringent so that technically almost all *collegia* in order to be *licita* needed the special *coire licet*. But there were numerous and conspicuous exceptions to this rule. The rule itself was based on the seditious character of many *collegia* which unless they were directly supervised by the state became prolific centres of agitation. But when the government found nothing objectionable in certain types of associations it relaxed its rule. Thus numerous colleges in the inscriptions which are undoubtedly authorized fail to reveal the special grant of *coire licet*. The *collegium fabrum* of the reign of Septimius Severus does not mention that it was specially authorized in any one of its inscriptions preserved to us.[35]

But two types of colleges, funerary (*collegia tenuiorum*) and industrial, certainly needed no special authorization. Marcian says : " But it is permitted to the *tenuiores* to contribute a monthly subscription provided, however, that they meet only once a month, lest under a pretext of this kind an unlicensed college arise."[36] That this right of assembly was granted *en bloc* to funerary associations is further revealed by the following *senatus-consultum* found on one of the inscriptions : " Kaput ex S(enatus) C(onsulto) Populi R(omani) : —Quibus, co(ire co)nvenire collegium—(que) habere liceat. Qui stipem menstruam conferre volen(t in fun)era, init collegium c(oeant co)nferendi causa, unde defuncti sepeliantur."[37] This inscription was found at Lanuvium ; that the *senatus consultum* cited refers to all funerary colleges is betrayed by the words, " Quibus coire convenire collegiumve habere liceat." Some scholars have inferred from this inscription that there were other types of *collegia tenuiorum* besides the funerary colleges.[38] They point to the fact that the *senatus consultum* includes only the paragraph (*Kaput*), dealing with funerary colleges, and neglects the others. This diversity would explain Marcian's silence on the aims of the *collegia tenuiorum* : the aims differed with different types of *collegia*. Another type of *collegia tenuiorum*, according to the same view, is revealed by the letter of Trajan on the *eranoi* of Amisus, a free city of Bithynia, which states that the object of these associations was mutual help.[39] The same scholars, in support of their view that the *collegia tenuiorum* differed, point to the statement of Tertullian that the Christian corporations employed their treasury to nourish as well as to bury their poor brethren.[40] But whatever the case may be here, it is clear that an important category of *collegia* was exempted from compliance with the rule demanding special authorization. It is no wonder, then, that associations all over the Empire found security and toleration under the guise of *collegia tenuiorum*. The Christians did so and it is a good venture that the devotees of Mithra were also originally organized as funerary colleges in which condition they needed no special authorization.[41] Waltzing suggests that the reason the special *coire licet* was not required from the *tenuiores* was that the Emperors did not fear sedition among the common people and the army on whom their own power was really based. This privilege, however, was denied the upper and middle classes, who alone constituted a threat to the principate in the opening years of its existence.[42] This principle when applied to the Jews left them in the more privileged class of the *tenuiores*, for from Cæsar's time they had been a bulwark of support to those of the Emperors who treated them well. Moreover, every synagogue had as an integral part a funerary association, or rather group devoted to the performance of the final rites over the dead body of the member.[43] On this ground alone then the Jewish synagogue would need no special *coire licet* to make it a *collegium licitum.* At least the funerary character of the Synagogue could in itself account for the one meeting a month prescribed as a limit by the Digest (*dum semel in mense coeant*).

The other meetings which the Synagogue had to conduct for religious purposes can be accounted for on either of two hypotheses, either acceptable in the writer's opinion. One hypothesis assumes that religious associations, like funerary associations, needed no special authorization. The basis for this view is Marcian in the Digest: " but for religious motives they are not prohibited from uniting provided, however, that through this means nothing is done in violation of the senate's decree forbidding *collegia illicita.*"[43a] Waltzing, however, rejects this unqualified grant as annihilating the provisions of the *Lex Julia* (which forbade religious meetings), and another provision which forbade veterans to unite for religious ends.[44] His own interpretation is that Marcian's statement is an amplification of the Digest's previous one which forbade funerary colleges to meet more than once a month; modifying the interdict to exclude religious meetings so that funerary colleges could meet more than once a month, provided the extra meetings were religious in character. Proof of this permission to hold extra meetings for religious purposes is the fact that the *collegium Dianæ et Antinoi* had two banquets a month and that a *collegium Lavini* of Lucania also met twice in June.[45] Whatever view one accepts as to the licensing of religious associations, for our purpose it is sufficient to admit that religious meetings did not need a special permit. It is clear at least that the lack of a special authorization did not necessarily make the synagogue less of a *collegium licitum,* for there were numerous exceptions to the Imperial rule which required the special grant of a licence to associations. In fact, from the second century on, the government permitted the establishment without authorization of large numbers of industrial and religious *collegia*.

(4) *Race as a condition of membership in the synagogue.*

The objection that the Jewish community was too exclusive in its conditions of membership to be a *collegium licitum* seems to be equally ill-founded. We do know of *collegia* with conditions of eligibility which closely parallel those for admission to the Jewish synagogue. Thus heredity appears as a condition of membership in a number of *collegia*.[46] At Nicopolis a religious college of the year 227 is responsible for an inscription with an enumeration of the members in which the name of the father is followed by that of his son.[47] Apparently it is a hereditary college. Among funerary colleges there is one inscription found at Rome which also seems to imply heredity : " sub hac condicione—ut liberi adlegantur."[48] Its date is A.D. 153. Still another inscription, that of *Curia Jovis* at Simithus in North Africa, also funerary in character, reveals some sort of hereditary membership. It deals with a municipal *curia* organized as a funerary college and apparently includes whole families who aid in the funeral rites.[49] These examples of hereditary colleges or *collegia* with heredity as a condition of eligibility can be multiplied for the fourth century particularly, when the state imposed heredity as a condition on most professional colleges.

Far then from its being true that the state did not

recognize *collegia licita* which had race as a condition of membership, it is certain that heredity (a very similar feature) came to be a not uncommon feature of the *collegia*. Furthermore, the colleges had a right to impose whatever conditions of membership they chose. These conditions usually had to be approved by the government. This was accomplished through the medium of the *statutes* which were the official laws of the *collegia*.[50] If the state approved them, there was nothing more to be said; the only condition the government imposed on these statutes was that they must not violate public law (*ius publicum privatorum pactis mutari non potest*).[51] In return the state undertook to see that these statutes were enforced by the members and to help punish infractions. The state itself often imposed additional conditions on the *collegia* as when Pliny found the number of 150 members rather small for a *collegium fabrum*.[52]

Some synagogues have " statutes."

The same situation applied to the Jewish synagogues. They also probably had their statutes. The Jewish community of Apamea for example possessed its νομος as probably did that of Rome, whose statutes, however, following the Latin usage were designated as *lex*.[53]

Possessing its own statutes then, the Jewish community needed but the approval of the government to become a *collegium licitum*. These statutes, moreover, included heredity as a condition of membership, and the government, in this case as in others, by approving the statutes, sanctioned the principle of heredity. In the light of the government's intervention in other *collegia* it is not strange also if it chose to impose certain conditions of its own on the Jewish synagogue. Such a condition might well be the obligation on the part of the synagogue to restrict the membership exclusively to members of one race.

(5) *Differences in extent of respective functions and jurisdictions of synagogues and collegia.*

A further difference between the synagogue and the *collegium* to which Juster attaches considerable importance is the difference in the complexity of their respective functions and in the extent of their jurisdictions. Juster sums it up by calling the Jewish organization a community with extended jurisdiction composed of numerous units as synagogues; and the *collegia* ordinary clubs with practically no jurisdiction over their members.

As regards jurisdiction undoubtedly there was some difference between the two, but not enough seriously to call into question the synagogue's possible organization as a *collegium licitum*. In the first place it should be clear that the assembly and officers of the *collegia licita* ordinarily possessed numerous judicial attributions. They decided in certain cases whether there was need of inflicting fixed fines on the membership and also possessed a system of eviction comparable to the excommunication of the Synagogue.[54] This jurisdiction, though not extensive, is essentially of the same type as that exercised by the Jewish community in Rome. We pointed out previously that there were fundamental differences between the Jewish communities in Italy, say, and those of Alexandria. These differences are nowhere so clearly revealed as in the question of their respective jurisdictions. In Alexandria, where most of the Jews were not Roman citizens, the Jewish authorities had the right to pass sentence for all sorts of infractions, sentences from which the Jews could not appeal to the ordinary civil authorities.[55] But in Italy, the Jews, because of the fact that they were Roman citizens, could appeal from this jurisdiction to the civil authorities.[56] The result was that the actual legal powers of the Jewish community in Rome came to amount to practically nothing. But since the community still preserved a religious and moral prestige it came to exercise a voluntary jurisdiction over many of its members. That is, the members would voluntarily often submit claims for settlement to the leaders of the community. The Jewish communal jurisdiction in a city like Rome became, therefore, a form of arbitration.[57] This is the "extra" jurisdiction which may obscure the essential negligibility of the *real* jurisdiction of the community and may blind one to the similarity in the functions of the synagogue and the *collegia licita*. There was, then, nothing compelling about the laws of either synagogue or *collegia*, but unwillingness to submit to them involved loss of membership, a conclusion few members desired ; so that a moral suasion was always operative to compel members to submit to the jurisdiction of one or the other. But this submission was entirely voluntary and limited in law.

(6) *Communal character of synagogue and collegia.*

The communal feature of the Jewish organization finds an exact parallel in that of the *collegia licita*. The

Digest reveals clearly that many *collegia* were modelled on the cities (*ad exemplum reipublicæ*).[58] The imitation is clear even in the words used to describe some of the typical phenomena of college life. Thus the reunion of all the members is called *populus*, or *ordo*, or sometimes *numerus*. Like citizens of the cities, the members of the colleges were often divided into centuries and these in turn into *decuries*. Following the system in the cities, *decuries* were often designated by numbers. Each century had its chief, a centurion with a lieutenant called an *optio*.[59] In the same way each decury was presided over by a *decurion*. The *decuries* were often independent units like the synagogues which formed the Jewish community. At Salome, for example, each decury of *fabri* had its own treasury (arca) and treasurer, just as each synagogue had its own reserve of funds.[60]

In its hierarchy of classes the city was also the model for the *collegia*. The city had its patrons, magistrates, its senate, and its *plebs*. It was the same for the colleges. Like the city the *collegium* had its general assembly called *conventus*, which was held in temples and met regularly in accordance with the requirements of the statutes.[61]

An interesting illustration of such a community *collegium* is found in an inscription at Simithus, which describes a municipal *curia* organized as a funerary college. The inscription is concerned with a number of measures designed to expedite and assure the burial of members. Fines were imposed for infractions such as lack of respect to the officers, failure to attend meetings or failure to help at funerals. Members of families especially were obliged to attend to the rites of deceased relatives under penalty of a fine. The *collegium* reveals a very extensive organization. Mention is made of such officers as *magister*, *flamen* and *quæstor*, each with some special sphere of competence.[62] In brief, the picture the *collegia* present to us as regards the form of internal organization is one of diversification and variety and the synagogue constituted no exception to this rule.

(7) *Membership in two associations.*

Marcian, in the Digest, is responsible for the following rule : " One may not belong to more than one *collegium licitum*."[63] Juster has argued that the presence within the Jewish community of colleges of artisans is explicable only on the assumption that the synagogue was not a *collegium licitum*. The case is not quite so simple, however. In the first place, many students have applied Marcian's interdict only to membership in two funerary colleges, for the clause cited occurs after the section on the funerary colleges and would therefore normally follow the context. In the second place those scholars who regard the interdict as not confined to funerary colleges do confine it to membership in two *collegia* having different aims.[64] It is only on the basis of some such explanation that one can account for the large number of instances in the inscriptions of men who belonged to two or more *collegia*.[65] In the light of these considerations it is probable that the rule of Marcian was enforced only when a positive need for it arose ; its purpose, it is worth noting, was to prevent the union of numerous *collegia* with the consequent danger of seditious agitation. This factor was not often operative in the case of the Jewish professional colleges and synagogues which really contained the same members and therefore as unions presented no novel combinations of political importance to the government.

V. *The synagogues become centres of unrest at times.*

But at times the Jewish synagogues probably did become centres of political unrest and under those circumstances it is not strange that the government should have dealt severely with them. Some such situation might well account for the occasional " suppressions " to which the Jews were subjected in the Empire, particularly at Rome. Unless we accept some such view this periodic persecution presents us with a problem which is extremely baffling. If Judaism was a *religio licita* and the synagogues *collegia licita*, why the persecutions under Tiberius and Claudius ? Mommsen urges his own solution of the question : that the persecutions were directed against Jewish Roman citizens who had failed to conform to the Roman cult. But the evidence for this view is lacking and we can explain the situation without assuming Judaism to have been a *religio illicita*.

In Roman legal usage there was a distinction between colleges which were simply unauthorised and those which were strictly illicit. The former, provided they were not dangerous, might even be tolerated ; they were not necessarily *collegia illicita*.[66] The latter term, however, was applied usually to colleges, authorized or not, which had acquired a dangerous character. It is in this sense that Marcian employs the term when he speaks of the *collegia tenuiorum* : " but the humble persons (*tenuiores*) are permitted to collect a monthly donation ;

provided, however, that they meet only once each month so that under this pretext they may not become an unlicensed college (*illicitum collegium*)."[67] It is in the same sense that an equivalent term is used by Trajan when he advises Pliny not to authorize at Nicomedia a college of *fabri* for fear " lest they become a *hetaireia*."[68]

Repressive measures under Tiberius and under Claudius.

It was probably because the synagogues had become *illicita* in the sense of disorderly that Tiberius and Claudius adopted restrictive measures against them. In the case of Tiberius, the measure reveals itself clearly as an administrative or police matter when taken together with other measures of a similar nature. Riots and agitation among the colleges led Tiberius to suppress the *collegia*. Tiberius' act was, therefore, an administrative, repressive one ; it did not touch on the legality or the illegality of the *collegia*. It was likely that Tiberius' efforts should also extend to putting down the Jewish synagogues which had also probably become centres of unrest. According to reports he sent 4,000 Jews off to Sardinia in military service.

With the fall of Sejanus, however, the Jews were reinstated in their former position. Tiberius' measure then was temporary and based on the turbulence of the Jewish synagogues which had thus become *collegia illicita*. It was not based on the illegality of the synagogues any more than the suppression of the *collegia* was based on the illegality of the latter.[69]

A similar line of argument applies to the persecution of the Jews under Claudius. Suetonius puts the blame for the whole matter squarely on the shoulders of the

Jews who had become riotous and finally brought down on themselves the Imperial edict of expulsion.[70] Dio, however, instead of an expulsion speaks of an interdict to unite, a prohibition that would have point when applied to *collegia* whose very existence at law hinged on the *coire licet*.[71] From the fact that no writers speak of the return of the Jews to Rome it is clear that Dio was probably correct in making Claudius' measure a simple interdict against Jewish associations, a measure which would strike equally well the cause of the trouble (turbulence in meetings). In other words here, as under Tiberius and even under the Republic, it was simply the fact of the Jewish synagogues becoming *illicita* in the sense of disorderly that brought down the intervention of the government. This intervention, furthermore, in its typical form, presupposed a collegiate organization in the Jewish community of Rome.

Conclusion.

In brief, then, on the basis of Josephus' specific evidence and the general similarity in the organization of the synagogues and the *collegia* we may feel justified in regarding the Jewish communities as *collegia licita*.

NOTES

[1] The general treatment of the *collegia* in this chapter is based mainly on J. Waltzing, *Corporations professionelles chez les Romains*, 4, v., Louvain, 1895–1900. Volumes 1 and 2 contain a historical study of the corporations. Volume 3 contains most of the Greek and Latin inscriptions dealing with *Collegia*; Volume 4 contains an index to the inscriptions.

(2) Dill, Samuel, *Roman Society from Nero to Marcus Aurelius*, p. 256, describes the role of the *collegia* in the social life of the Empire.

(3) In fact the Roman law strictly knew no *religio licita* but only *collegia licita*.

(4) Among others, Harnack in his *Entstehung und Entwicklung der Kirchenverfassung und des Kirchenrechts in den zwei ersten Jahrhunderten*, Leipzig, 1910, follows the lead of Renan in regarding the Jewish communities as associations.

(5) Jos., *Ant.*, XIV, 10, 8.

(6) Philo, *Leg. Ad. Gaium*, 24 (Ed. Cohn, 1915).

(7) *Les Juifs*, I, 413–424.

(8) *Dig.*, XVII, 2, 70 : " Nulla societatis in aeternum coitio est."

(9) Waltzing, *Corporations professionelles*, I, 340.

(10) Terms like *corpus* or *universitas* are frequently used to describe the Jewish community. See Juster, I, ch. IV, *passim*.

(11) *Ant.*, XIV, 10, 8.

(12) Livy, 39, 18 : " neu qua pecunia communis . . . esset." C. I. L., I, p. 196, L. 10 : " Neve Pecuniam quis quam eorum comoinem habuisse velet."

(13) Cf., however, Waltzing, Art. " Collegia," *Dict. d'arch. chrét.*, fasc. XXXI, cols. 2113 *seq.*

(14) Tertullian, *Apologeticus*, 38 ff.

(15) Juster, I, 438–456.

(16) Juster, I, 424–438.

(17) *Dig.*, 34, 5, 20, 12.

(18) *Corp. Jur.*, I, 9, 1 : " Imp. Antoninus A. Claudius Tryphoniano, Quod Cornelia Salvia Universitati Judaeorum qui in Antiochensium civitate constituti sunt, legavit, peti non potest, D. Prid. Kal. Iul. Antonino A. IIII et Balbino Conss."

(19) Juster, I, 486, note.

(20) Juster, I, 434.

[21] Juster discards the solution, *op. cit.*, I, 432. Cuq's view is not accepted by most scholars : It is offered here as a likely hypothesis.

[22] " Funus," by E. Cuq, *Dictionnaire des antiquités grecques et romaines.*

[23] This has been urged on the basis of Philo, *De Josepho,* 43, *De spec. legib,* 3, 5, who says that in accordance with the Mosaic law the prostitute was to be stoned to death. This view is espoused by Goodenough in his recent book *Jewish Law Courts at Alexandria,* New Haven, 1929, pp. 25, 33, who maintains that the Romans countenanced the situation unofficially. However, in the light of the less rigorous system in Palestine, Philo's remark was probably theoretical. Juster, II, 157, takes up the matter fully.

[24] Cf. *infra.*

[25] For example, immunity from degrading punishments. Cf. the case of Saul of Tarsus, *Acts,* 18 : 12.

[26] *Op. cit.,* I, 417–424.

[27] The two central institutions of greatest importance were the *Patriarchate* and the *Sanhedrin.* The latter was, naturally, mainly a local Palestine institution with a correspondingly circumscribed jurisdiction. The Partiarch was in the later period (3rd century) a sort of hereditary Jewish leader in the East recognized by the Romans.

[28] But we do not wish to be construed as hinging our position on the status of the Jewish communities in the East ; we are specially concerned with the Western Jewish communities which we have no doubt were *collegia licita,* and we are merely adverting now and again to the Eastern situation to fill out (hypothetically and problematically, perhaps), the general background and connection of the Jewish position in the West. It is worth noting, however, that the organization of the Tyrians in Puteoli, known as *Consistentes,* had a quasi-national character. This was unusual in the West. See art. " Consistentes," in *Pauly-Wissowa, Real Encyclopädie.*

[29] Juster, I, 424.

[30] Juster, apparently without excuse, rules out the evidences for the existence of Jewish statutes, and the affirmative opinion of S. Reinach (*Rev. des et. juives*, 7 : 161), in connection with the " nomos " of Apamea (Reinach believes this " nomos " is a typical collegium statute). Cf. Juster, I, 424.

[31] Juster, I, 424.

[32] Juster, *Ibid.*

[33] Juster, I, 485, note 4.

[34] Waltzing, *Corporations professionelles*, I, 81.

[35] Waltzing, *Cor. prof.*, I, 130 : *Corpus Inscriptionum Latinarum*, III, 1043, 1051.

[36] *Dig.*, 47, 22 : " Sed permittitur tenuioribus stipem menstruam conferre dum tamen semel in mense coeant ne sub praetextu hujusmodi illicitum collegium coeat."

[37] *C. I. L.*, XIV, 2112.

[38] Wallon, H., *L'esclavage dans l'antiquité*, 3 v., Paris, 1897, III, 462.

[39] Pliny, *Ep.*, 92–93.

[40] *Apologet*, 39. This assumes that the Christians were organized in funerary colleges, which is vehemently disputed by P. Batiffol, *L'Eglise naissante*, p. 41 ; by J. Zeiller, *L'Empire romain et l'église*, p. 46, and by Waltzing in *Dictionnaire d'archéolgie et de liturgie chrétienne*, fasc. XXXI, col. 2113 *seq.* In affirmative, see Boissier, *Rel. Rom.*, II, 30.

[41] Cumont, Franz, *Les Mystéres de Mithra*, Brussels, 1913, p. 86, however, prefers the view that the followers of Mithra originally enjoyed protection by virtue of their union with the cult of *Magna Mater*.

[42] Waltzing, *Corp. prof.*, I, 149.

[43] See the fragment of Hecataeus of Abdera preserved in Diodorus Siculus 40, 3 (Reinach, *Textes relatifs au Judaisme*, p. 19) ; Tacitus, *Hist.*, 5, 5. For the general discussion ee Juster, I, 480 ff.

153

[43a] Quoted by Waltzing, *Corp. prof.*, I, 152–153 : " Sed religionis causa coire non prohibentur, dum tamen per hoc non fiat contra senatus consultum, quo illicita collegia arcentur."

[44] *Dig.*, 47, 112 : " Sub praetextu religionis vel sub specie solvendi voti coetus illicitos nec a veteranis temptari oportet." Waltzing, *Corp. prof.*, I, 152–153.

[45] *C. I. L.*, XIX, 2112 ; X, 444.

[46] Cf. Waltzing, *Corp. prof.*, IV, 258.

[47] *C. I. L.*, III, 6150.

[48] *C. I. L.*, VI, 10234.

[49] *C. I. L.*, VIII, 14, 683.

[50] These statutes are known by various designations. The following may suffice to give some idea of the diversity of nomenclature : *Pactio* (*Dig.*, 47, 22, 4) ; *Lex.* (*C. I. L.*, VI, 10234) ; *Conventio* (*C. I. L.*, X, 1579).

[51] *Dig.* (Papinian), II, 14, 38.

[52] Juster, I, 424 : Ramsay, *Cities of Phrygia*, No. 399.

[53] *C. I. L.*, X, 1893 : (the inscription of Pouzzoles) : " Praeter legem ne quis mihi titulum deiciat curam agatur."

[54] *C. I. L.*, X, 1579 ; XI, 10298 ; XIV, 2112.

[55] This was undoubtedly true in Palestine till the year A.D. 70, both in the civil and in the penal spheres, though the right of inflicting capital punishment was restricted. See Juster, II, 127, for bibliographies and critical treatment.

[56] Jewish courts in the Diaspora had no real penal jurisdiction except in some of the older Hellenistic centres. An example of the latter is contained in Jos., *Ant.*, XIV, 10, 2, where Caesar gives the Jewish Ethnarch of Palestine jurisdiction in matters of religious custom even over communities of the Greek Diaspora.

[57] The proquaestor of Jos., *Ant.*, XIV, 10, 17, for example, gives the Jewish Roman citizens of Sardis a *right* to their courts. It is significant that the same *right* was enjoyed by non-Jews, of bringing complaints to Jewish tribunals. The jurisdiction in neither case was more than voluntary.

[58] *Dig.*, III, 4, 1.

[59] *C. I. L.*, V, 5738, 5701.

[60] *C. I. L.*, III, 2107.

[61] *C. I. L.*, VI, 10234; III, 924.

[62] *C. I. L.*, VIII, 14, 683.

[63] *Dig.*, 47, 22 : " Non licet autem amplius quam unum collegium
licitum habere."

[64] Waltzing, *Corp. prof.*, I, 149.

[65] At Ostia, a Tiber boatman was a wheat merchant and president
of the bakers, *C. I. L.*, XIV, 4234; for other illustrations
see XII, 1898; XIV, 2, 309.

[66] They were simply " collegia quibus non coire licet."

[67] *Digest*, 47, 22 : " Sed permittitur tenuioribus stipem menstruam
conferre, dum tamen semel in mense coeant ne sub praetextu
hujusmodi illicitum collegium coeant."

[68] Pliny, *Ep.*, 33–34.

[69] The expulsion of the Jews in A.D. 19 has been a favourite
subject of investigation among scholars. The sources for
the incident are Josephus, *Ant.*, XVIII, 3, 5 ; Tacitus, *Ann.*,
II, 85 ; Suet. *Tib.*, 36 ; Philo, *Leg. ad Caium*, 24 ; Seneca,
Ep., 108, 22 ; Dio Cas., LVII, 18. The most important of
these sources are Josephus and Tacitus. Suetonius and Dio
Cassius are apparently based on the latter. In Tacitus' jejeune
account the incident is connected with public morality and
is appropriately linked with the expulsion of the Egyptian
devotees. The 4,000 sent to Sardinia are described by Tacitus
as *generis libertini*. This term has been taken by Merrill to
include only a special class of freedmen and their descendants.
He cites another case of its use in Tacitus in a similar sense.
He concludes from this and other considerations that only a
section of the Jewish population was affected, that Jews in
possession of the complete *civitas* were not touched. Josephus'
version also links the Isiac scandal with the Jewish troubles.
According to him it was the activity of two imposters
soliciting funds for " hangings for the Temple " that provoked

the government's intervention. Josephus' account has always puzzled scholars : how could an incident of such trifling importance produce such a drastic measure as expulsion ? It appears that Josephus was trying to conceal something. What ? W. A. Heidel has suggested a plausible though startling answer. Arguing from the connection of the incident with the Isiac scandal in which a distinguished Roman matron had been tricked into prostitution by an admirer in the guise of the god Anubis, and from the connotation of the expression " Temple hangings " he argues that the two Jews or imposters were soliciting *hierodules* for the Jewish temple. It is not our purpose to criticize any of these views but one feature both in Josephus' and Tacitus' account and the modern construc- tions of them stands out—that it was simply temporary motives that inspired the Roman government's policy of repression and that Mommsen's view that this repression was due to the fact that Jewish Roman citizens were practising an unlicensed cult, is without basis. See the following articles. E. T. Merrill, " Expulsion of Jews from Rome under Tiberius," *Classical Philology*, 14 : 365–72 (1919); W. A. Heidel, " Why Were Jews Banished from Italy in 19 A.D. ? " *Am. Journ. Philol.*, 41 : 38–47 (1920).

(70) Suetonius, *Claudius*, 25, 4 : " Judaeos impulsore chresto assidue tumultuantis Roma expulit."

(71) Dio Cas., 60, 6, 6. Other sources for the Claudian " expulsion " are *Orosius*, 7, 6, 15, and *Acts*, 18 : 2. Do these sources record two different " expulsions " ? See Reinach, *Rev. des ét. juives*, 1895, tome XXXI, p. 161–178 ; Leclercq, art. " Judaisme," *Dict. d'arch. chrét.*, fasc. LXXX, cols. 153–154.

CHAPTER VII

CONCLUSION

WE spoke at the beginning of the work of the thread that unites the elements of our problem and renders desirable some explanation based on the public law. The thread that provides this explanation exists in the Roman principles of citizen and religious exclusiveness. Inspired by these principles, Rome prosecuted in turn pagan religions and Christianity. In most cases the official *pretext* for the state's action was that these religions were foreign and unauthorized. On the other hand Rome tolerated and even encouraged Judaism and Isis, but true to the principle of religious exclusiveness, she regulated them to fit more easily into the fabric of the state. The *form* of the picture is undoubtedly unitary and Roman.

The following conclusions, then, seem to the author defensible :

1. Foreign and unauthorised pagan cults were suppressed, sometimes because they were disorderly, sometimes because they were practised by Roman citizens.

2. The procedure in such cases was based on either the regular criminal law or the *coercitio* (discretionary authority) of the magistrate.

3. Christianity enjoyed toleration at first because it

157

was identified with Judaism. When it ceased to be so identified it was prosecuted, in some cases because it was not a religion authorized for citizens; in some cases because it refused to accommodate itself to the imperial cult. Neither monotheism nor default of nationality was directly responsible for the action of the government.

4. The procedure employed against the Christian cult was based on either of the following spheres of criminal action : (a) The regular criminal law involving the charges of *maiestas*, *sacrilegium*, or the *nomen Christianum* ; or even the *flagitia*, or crimes, reputed to adhere to the *nomen Christianum* ; (b) The *coercitio* of the magistrate.

5. Judaism was a national cult in Palestine and a quasi-national cult in the Hellenistic cities of the East. Its position in Palestine was based on the old *fœdus* or treaty with Rome and its position in the eastern Greek cities was based on the dispositions of the Hellenistic rulers, subsequently confirmed by Rome.

6. Judaism was a *religio licita*, or authorized religion, and its synagogues *collegia licita*, or authorized associations, in the western parts of the Roman Empire, such as Italy, Spain, and Gaul, where Jews enjoyed Roman citizenship in large numbers.

But when we inquire as to the *causes* that led to the toleration of Judaism and the persecution of Christianity we run into the realm of accident as well as of law. If Tiberius, as Tertullian relates,[1] had carried through his project of having Christianity admitted to the state a sanguinary chapter would be missing in Roman history, but he would have anticipated by three centuries the close of the classical civilization.

The end of the ancient state coincides with the

triumph of Christianity. The triumph of Christianity marks the close of the political and religious development of the classical civilization. The dichotomy between church and state which characterizes society since the fourth century makes its appearance in the last age of the Roman Empire. " Render unto Cæsar what is Cæsar's and unto God what is God's," is a rule which the ancient state knew not and could hardly acknowledge.

This is not merely a coincidence ; it is a sequence, as Fustel de Coulanges has pointed out.[2] The close integration of the ancient gods with the classical community was of the essence of the life of the ancient civilization. When this link disappeared the vital part of the clasical culture went with it.

There has, of course, always been a relationship between religion and politics. In modern times, as Figgis has pointed out, religious tolerance was the parent of political liberty. In the ancient world it may be argued that political freedom, at least municipal freedom, was the parent or the progenitor of religious liberty. The line between religious and political persecution, however, is clear in most cases. Religious persecution is based on religious convictions entertained either by the victim or the oppressor. Political persecution is grounded in political notions accepted by either or both of the principal parties. If occasionally the line between these two types of intolerance gets blurred that is no argument against the existence of such a line.

If a comparison is made between ancient and modern conceptions on this subject it will reveal some interesting points of difference as well as similarity. On the whole, Roman persecution of religious groups where it existed was essentially political. The medieval opposition to dissenting groups or individuals was avowedly religious. The modern theory is political and strangely reminiscent of the antique view. The modern separation of the secular and the religious has not prevented a certain amount of confusion between things that are purely religious and those purely political. Thus a great part of the Roman opposition to the early Christians was based on the refusal of that group to participate in the cult of the Emperor or the cult of the gods. The persecution was religious so far as it was based on the cult; it was political, however, to a greater extent, because it was based also on the violation of the patriotic ceremonies of the Empire. Modern persecution of dissenting cults is never avowedly anchored in religious intolerance but, what almost amounts to the same thing, is a product of civism or the religion of nationalism. The imperial cult in the Empire and the salute to the flag in a modern country both have the characteristics of religious ceremonies, but both pretend to be political acts dictated and required by the community in its secular rather than in its religious capacity.

In both ancient and modern polities there is a problem of the relationship of the state and the individual which runs over into the religious sphere. In both, political liberty may become religious liberty and religious liberty may become political liberty.

NOTES

[1] *Apol.*, V, 2.

[2] *La Cité antique*, Paris, 1923, pp. 456-457.